OKiDOKi

FiT iN ...

Englisch

für den Abschluss nach Klasse 10

Schroedel

OKiDOKi FiT iN Englisch
für den Abschluss nach Klasse 10

Jens Bolhöfer
Cordula Dopichei
Hyacinth Moodalie-Hünnemeyer
Anke Strauß

unter Mitarbeit von Richard Horne
und Nickolas Woods

Bibliografische Information Der Deutschen Bibliothek
Die Deutsche Bibliothek verzeichnet diese Publikation in der Deutschen Nationalbibliografie; detaillierte bibliografische Daten sind im Internet über http://dnb.ddb.de abrufbar.

Nach gültiger Rechtschreibung 2006

ISBN 978-3-507-**22272**-4
alt: 3-507-**22272**-8

Lektorat: Dr. Stephan Schmal
Layout: Janssen Kahlert Design & Kommunikation, Hannover
Illustrationen: Dietmar Griese, Laatzen
Satz und Lithos: KCS GmbH, Buchholz/Hamburg
Druck und Bindung: pva, Landau 09/06

OKiDOKi stellt sich vor

OKiDOKi FiT iN Englisch bietet eine Vielzahl von Übungen zur Verbesserung der **sprachlichen Mittel** an und trägt bei zum intensiven Training der Grundkompetenzen **Sprechen**, **Lesen** und **Schreiben**.
Damit wird der Unterrichtsstoff der Jahrgangsstufen 7 bis 10 wiederholt und eine optimale Vorbereitung auf den **Abschluss der 10. Klasse** gewährleistet.

An wen richtet sich Okidoki? An alle,
- die durch selbstständiges Arbeiten ihre Schulnoten verbessern wollen
- die bereits vorhandenes Wissen auffrischen möchten
- die Spaß daran haben, Neues zu lernen

Okidoki hat am Ende des Buches den praktischen Lösungsteil.

Die folgenden Elemente begleiten dich beim Lernen und sorgen für Überblick:

TIPP Im Tipp findest du Regeln, Hilfen und Merksätze verständlich formuliert.

ÜBUNGSTIPP Im Übungstipp gibt es praktische Hinweise zum Arbeiten und wie du dir das Lernen erleichtern kannst.

ACHTUNG Hier wirst du auf besonders schwierige Regeln, Ausnahmen und andere Dinge hingewiesen, die du dir besonders merken musst.

TEST Jeweils am Ende der Hauptkapitel findest du einen Test, mit dem du selbstständig deinen Lernerfolg überprüfen kannst. Testen sollst du deine Fähigkeiten auch vor und nach der Arbeit mit diesem Buch (Einstiegstest und Abschlusstest).

Aufgaben mit diesem Zeichen musst du in deinem Heft oder auf einem Extrablatt lösen.

INHALT

OKiDOKi stellt sich vor 3

Einstiegstest: Was kann ich schon? 6

Kapitel 1: Lesen 6

Grundvoraussetzungen 10
Informative texts / factual texts 11
appeal, travel guide, film review
Literature / poetry 20
Robert Hayes: Protest of a Sixth Former

Literature / diary 22
Sue Townsend: The Diary of Adrian Mole
Literature / novel 23
J. Gaarder: Sophie's World
Fable 25
J. Thurber: The Owl who was God
Urban legend 29
The perfect Mousse

Test Lesen – Das kann ich jetzt 32

Kapitel 2: Schreiben 34

Allgemeine Hinweise zum Schreiben 34
Writing an email 34
Writing informal and formal letters 35
letter of application
Writing a CV (Curriculum Vitae) 37
Writing a summary 38
Isaac Asimov: The fun they had
Writing a diary entry 41
Creative writing 42
T. Jones: The Meeting
Writing a missing part of a story or an ending, Writing a dialogue
Comment writing 46
Writing a review (Kritik) 46
W. Allen: Matchpoint
Comment on a picture 48
Adolph von Menzel: "French Window" and Edward Hopper: "Nighthawks"
Useful phrases and expressions for writing 50

Test Schreiben – Das kann ich jetzt 52

Kapitel 3: Sprechen ... 54

Grundvoraussetzungen ... 54
Getting ready for a discussion ... 55
Gesprächsfelder ... 57
Talking about TRAVEL, Talking about FASHION, Talking about CAR TRAFFIC
Fragen im Gespräch ... 61
Telephone language ... 62
Getting ready for a presentation ... 63

Test Sprechen – Das kann ich jetzt ... 66

Kapitel 4: Grammatik ... 68

Parts of speech – Wortarten ... 68
prefixes, suffixes, simple present, present progressive
Tenses – Zeitformen ... 70
simple present, present progressive
Expressing the future ... 72
will-future, going-to-future, present progressive, simple present, future progressive, future perfect
Past tenses ... 75
simple past, simple present perfect, present perfect progressive, past perfect
Modal auxiliaries ... 81
Special verb forms ... 83
gerunds, infinitives, participles
Adjectives – adverbs ... 87
Word order ... 90
Satztypen ... 91
conjunctions, prepositions, relative clauses, conditional sentences, reported speech (indirect speech)
Passive voice ... 99

Test Grammatik – Das kann ich jetzt ... 101

Abschlusstest: Was habe ich gelernt? ... 105

Some common mistakes ... 108
Lösungen ... 110

Anke Strauß und **Cordula Dopichei** haben langjährige Unterrichtserfahrung im Fach Englisch. Sie sind in der Lehrerbildung tätig und haben bei verschiedenen Englisch-Lehrwerken beratend und als Autorinnen mitgewirkt. **Hyacinth Moodalie-Hünnemeyer** ist englische Muttersprachlerin und bringt internationale Lehrerfahrung an Schule und Hochschule mit, **Jens Bolhöfer** ist Dezernent am Niedersächsischen Landesamt für Lehrerbildung und Schulentwicklung (NiLS).
Übrigens: OKiDOKi freut sich über Post. E-Mail: okidoki@schroedel.de
Du kannst OKiDOKi auch im Internet besuchen: www.okidoki.de

Runaways

Bink's story

Bink, 15, from London, ran away from home when she was 12. "I still don't know why I ran away. My mum believes it was because my brother had been going through a difficult time and I wanted some attention. Maybe that's true, but if so, it was entirely subconscious.

Whatever the reason, I found myself outside the local cemetery at 3am on a Sunday waiting for dawn. When the gates were unlocked, I hid a bag I'd packed and my sleeping bag behind a bush. Then I spent the rest of the day walking around and sitting in the bus shelter. At dusk I went back to the cemetery, hid until the gates were locked, and settled on the ground below the bush. After a good cry, I slept despite the rain and the heat-seeking police helicopters flying overhead – whose mission I never suspected.

The next evening I saw something in the street which shocked and terrified me – a placard advertising my disappearance. I took a page from my Post Office book and wrote a message on it to my family, intending to pin it up at school. But on the way I bumped into my violin teacher, who had no idea I had been reported missing. We chatted and then I headed off to find somewhere to sleep. But when she reached the main street and saw the placard, she telephoned the police and came to find me.

As soon as I returned home and found everyone worried sick I saw the consequences of running away. However it was a long time before I fully came to terms with how selfish I'd been."

Vocabulary:
subconscious – unbewusst
cemetery – Friedhof

Stuart's story

"There were all sorts of dodgy people hanging about. I was relieved when the police took me to the station."

Stuart, 16.

Middlesex teenager Stuart was 15 when he first ran away from home after tensions between him and his mother's new boyfriend became unbearable.

After fare-dodging his way to Bournemouth on the train he found a night shelter – which called social services because he was under-age.

His mother came to collect him but after he returned the arguments became worse. So he fled to London, where he slept rough in Tottenham Court Road tube station.

"It was pretty scary," he says. "There were all sorts of dodgy people hanging about. I was relieved when the police took me to the station."

Once he turned 16, Stuart left home and is living in a hostel run by London homeless charity Centerpoint. He hopes to have his own place soon.

Vocabulary:
relieved – erleichtert
fare-dodging – schwarzfahren
tube – Schlauch, *hier:* U-Bahn
sleep rough – obdachlos übernachten
scary – furchterregend
dodgy – zwielichtig, unseriös

Simon's story

"I get on a lot better with my mum now that I'm not at home." Simon left home last year as soon as he turned 16. But it was when he was 15 and hanging around with a bad crowd who'd been suspended from school, that he decided to run away from his home in Wakefield.

"I was in trouble with the police, and there were constant rows in the house," he remembers. "So I stayed round at a friend's place. I talked to my mates, but they didn't know what I should do, so I went to see a social worker. She sorted out somewhere for me to stay." Simon is now living in supported accommodation provided by Barnardo's, a charity which helps disadvantaged children to improve their chance in life.

"I feel I've learned a lot on my own," he says. "I know how to look after myself. I'm a lot more independent. I get on a lot better with my mum now that I don't live at home. It's a bit sad, but that's life."

Vocabulary:
row – *hier:* Streit, Aufruhr
supported accommodation – betreute Wohneinrichtung
charity – Wohltätigkeitsverein

What makes you run ?

People see runaways as bad kids who waste police time, yet many don't take the decision lightly. The main reasons they give for running are:

1. Problems at home: arguments with mum and dad; being abused; feeling ignored or resenting a step-parent.
2. Worries at school: being bullied; facing exams; unfair treatment by a teacher; pressure to succeed.
3. Depression and anger: falling out with a boy/girlfriend; hitting back at family who've upset you.
4. Need to hide from: drugs; trouble with police; revealing pregnancy.
5. Boredom: crave adventure and attention to liven up regular routine.

Vocabulary:
waste time – Zeit verschwenden
resent – ablehnen
fall out with s.o. – sich mit jemandem verkrachen
hit back at s.o. – es jemandem heimzahlen
upset s.o. – jemanden sehr ärgern, „niedermachen"
pregnancy – Schwangerschaft

The facts

- An estimated 100,000 people under the age of 16 run away or are forced to leave home or care every year.
- Boys are more likely than girls to run away before the age of 11. But after the age of 14 girls are twice as likely to disappear.
- One in seven runaways spends a week or more away from home.
- Some "sofa-surf"(switching from friend to friend); some are picked up by strangers; about a quarter end up sleeping rough in back alleys, fields, parks and bus and train stations.
- There are only two refuges in the UK which provide shelter for people under the age of 16 – The Leeds Safe House and the Centrepoint NSPCC Refuge for Young Runaways in London.
- But you can't just turn up and expect to stay. There is a total of just 13 beds in the shelters – nothing compared to the 2,500 calls the charity Childline received 1998/9 from teenagers in need of somewhere to sleep.
- Many runaways said running gave them time to think and relief from pressure. But the longer a person stays away the greater the risk.

- The streets aren't always safe. One in seven children are assaulted while on the run; two thirds of young people who stay with a stranger will be attacked.
- Some turn to begging, rummaging in dustbins and selling sex or drugs.
- You're more likely to run if your mum and dad have split up or divorced, you live as part of a step-family or someone close to you has died.

(Judith Wood in: The Daily Telegraph, 4 March 2000; Copyright Telegraph Group Limited, 2000)

Vocabulary:
refuge – Zufluchtsort; hier: Anlaufstelle (für obdachlose Jugendliche)
assault – (tätlich) angreifen
rummage – kramen, wühlen
dustbin – Mülleimer

1. *Conditional sentences: With the help of the information given in text 1 (Bink's story), complete the sentences using the conditional.*

a) If Bink's brother hadn't been going through a difficult time, Bink ...

b) If Bink hadn't seen a placard advertising her disappearance, she ...

c) If her violin teacher hadn't seen the placard after having talked to her, she ...

d) If the police hadn't found him, Bink ...

2. *Reported Speech: Rewrite the following paragraph into reported speech.*

"I still don't know why I ran away. My mum believes it was because my brother had been going through a difficult time and I wanted some attention. Maybe that's true, but if so, it was entirely subconscious."

Start like this:

Bink said ...

3. *Questions: What questions might a reporter have asked Bink when interviewing her? Read the text again and ask 6 of the reporter's questions.*

4. *Writing.*

a) Write a summary of Bink's story in 80 to 100 words.

b) Imagine Stuarts future and write 100 words about it.

c) Comment on the following statement in about 250 words.

Society should offer help to runaways if their parents are not able or willing to bring up their children.

Grundvoraussetzungen

Kaum etwas stärkt das Sprachverständnis und die Vertrautheit mit der fremden Kultur so sehr wie der Umgang mit der Literatur. Das anfängliche Gefühl der Überforderung schwindet meist rasch, denn grundsätzlich gilt, dass man zum Verständnis von Texten nicht jedes Wort verstehen muss. Vieles lässt sich durch den Kontext erraten. Selbst wenn man sich bei der Übersetzung eines Begriffs nicht ganz sicher ist, wird man zumeist verstehen, worum es in dem Text geht.

Kommt es dem Leser darauf an, schnell die Hauptaussage eines Textes zu verstehen, verwendet man die so genannte ***Skimming***-Technik *(reading for gist).* Hierzu überfliegt man den Text, ohne dabei jedes einzelne Wort verstehen zu müssen. Allein wenn man die wichtigsten Wörter eines Satzes verstanden hat (Subjekt, Prädikat, Objekt), erfasst man die Hauptaussage des Textes. Diese Technik wendet man z. B. an, wenn man einen Zeitungsartikel schnell verstehen möchte.

Anders ist es beim so genannten ***Scanning***. Auch hierbei wird ein Text zügig gelesen, jedoch um gezielt bestimmte Informationen zu entnehmen *(reading for detail).* Wenn dir das Buch gehört, markierst du am besten die Schlüsselwörter *(keywords).* Scanning bietet sich z. B. an, wenn man einen Fahrplan oder Informationsbroschüren liest, bei der nur bestimmte Teile für den Leser von Interesse sind.

Bei allen Texten, ob fiktional oder nicht fiktional, sollte man darauf achten, warum und für wen sie geschrieben wurden. Häufig wird nämlich nicht offen (explizit) gesagt, welche Haltung der Autor zu dem Thema hat. Auch Nachrichten enthalten häufig neben den reinen Fakten implizite und damit interpretierende Aussagen, die bereits Stellung zum Thema beziehen und somit den Leser beeinflussen. Deshalb muss der Leser auf diese impliziten Äußerungen *(underlying message)* achten.

Topic: RUNNING AWAY – Fact Sheet

How many run away?

- 6,000–7,000 children under 16 run away every year for the first time.
- 9,000 run away each year, including those who run away more than once.

Who runs away?

- Running away is a teenage phenomenon but approximately one in five run before the age of 11.
- There is little difference in the rates of running away between urban, town and rural areas and similarly little difference between different ethnic groups.

The risks of running

- Around one-sixth of young people who run away are at risk of being either physically or sexually assaulted.
- Over a quarter will sleep rough on at least one occasion.
- One-third will stay with friends and a quarter with relatives.
- Approximately one in seven will have to steal and/or beg in order to survive.

Why do children and young people run away?

- To get away from arguments and conflict with parents or step-parents (or guardians)
- Abuse or neglect
- To escape and gain respite from conflict between parents or parents' problems such as drug/alcohol dependency
- Personal problems such as depression, loneliness and anxieties about the future, coping with bereavement, peer influences, trouble with the police or alcohol and drug use
- School difficulties such as bullying, truancy and fear of parental reaction, academic problems. Running away is closely associated with difficulties at school.

What children and young people say would help

- Accessible information about local advice and support services need to be available in places where children and young people meet.
- Advice counselling and family mediation before or at the time of running away – particularly help during divorce, separation, and persistent family conflict. Also help for parents who misuse drugs and alcohol.
- School-based preventive services including discussions about problems in family life
  - 'Refuges' for those under 16 which would allow them the time and space needed before taking the next step.
  - More and better supported emergency accommodation for 16/17 year olds with no stable home base.

(Extract from Vulnerable Children and Young People, Young Runaways (slightly adapted), Published by Scottish Executive St. Andrew's House, Edinburgh; Crown copyright 2003, ISBN 0-7559-0843-0)

Vocabulary:
vulnerable – verwundbar, empfindlich
sleep rough – auf der Straße leben, obdachlos sein
gain respite – Aufschub/Bedenkzeit gewinnen
bereavement – schmerzlicher Verlust
truancy – Schulschwänzen
refuge – Rückzugsraum, Schutzort

TIPP

Sachtexte haben meist einen informierenden oder appellierenden Charakter und beschreiben in der Regel Fakten. Man liest sie meistens, um bestimmte Informationen zu erhalten. Flugblätter und Broschüren sind eine besondere Art von Sachtexten. Sie haben fast immer den Anspruch, andere Menschen von etwas zu überzeugen. Deshalb sind sie häufig so aufgemacht, dass sie eine bestimmte Zielgruppe ansprechen und die Message schnell herüberbringen. Um dieses Ziel zu erreichen, bedienen sie sich einer entsprechend gewählten Sprache (register: formal or colloquial), *z. B. Umgangssprache* (colloquial, slang), *wenn sie Jugendliche ansprechen wollen.*

The following text is an extract from a "leaflet" from the British organisation SHELTER which helps the homeless. It is an appeal for donations for "Winterwatch", an initiative to help the homeless during the cold winter months.

Shelter
THE NATIONAL CAMPAIGN FOR HOMELESS PEOPLE

Your gift now could help us save people's lives this Winter!

The Winter Nights appeal is a response to Shelter's increasing concern for the thousands of people who are homeless – or living in damp, decaying homes not worthy of the name – during the winter months. They can be at the mercy of rain, snow and the freezing cold.

Sometimes the conditions they live in can kill. Winterwatch, an initiative we launched together with the charity Crisis, aims to create enough emergency accommodation across the country, so that no one is left without a bed in cold weather.

Our 40 Housing Aid Centres around the country help people living in appalling conditions to fight for decent housing, and also help people threatened with the prospect of losing their homes.

Our Nightline emergency telephone advice line gives vital help to desperate and homeless people who might otherwise spend nights on the freezing streets.

We simply can't let these things happen. So please, give what you can to our Winter Nights appeal today – and help us to prevent suffering and death in the cold winter nights ahead.

Thank you.

Homeless and desperate on the freezing city streets ...

Shelly had been beaten up by her partner, again, and she was desperate. It was midnight, freezing cold, and she had nowhere to go.

Standing in a call box, with her little girl Kate by her side, she managed to get through to Shelter's Nightline ... who found them both a bed in an emergency hostel. Now they're safe and warm, in a flat of their own.

Vocabulary:
increase – ansteigen, wachsen
decay – verfallen, verrotten
be at the mercy of s.th. – von der Gnade von etwas abhängen
appal – erschrecken, schockieren
prospect – Aussicht, Möglichkeit
desperate – auswegslos, verzweifelt, hoffnungslos

ÜBUNGSTIPP

Wenn du in einem Text einen Satz nicht auf Anhieb verstehst, schau dir die umliegenden Begriffe an. Selbst wenn dir keine Übersetzung für ein Wort oder einen Begriff einfällt, kannst du den Satz meistens aus seinem Kontext heraus verstehen. Manchmal geben auch die grammatischen Formen Aufschluss über die mögliche Bedeutung von Begriffen. Wenn du den Text aber auch nach mehrmaligem Lesen nicht verstehst, schlage die Wörter in einem Wörterbuch nach.

1. *Read the texts on p. 62–63 (Running away) and p. 64 (Shelter).*

2. *Comprehension / Understanding the texts: Answer the following questions in complete sentences. Try to use your own words as much as possible.*

TEXT A (Running away)
a. What are some of the risks young runaways face?
b. What type of school problems could lead a young person to run away from home?

TEXT B (Shelter)
a. Why was "Winterwatch" launched?
b. Describe the homes that the recipients seeking emergency accommodation are living in?

3. *Language and Vocabulary: Match the words and expressions in column 1 with those taken from the texts in column 2.*

COLUMN 1	COLUMN 2
a) on average	1. approximately
b) available	2. increasing
c) abuse	3. accessible
d) earn	4. accommodation
e) especially	5. vulnerable
f) appalling	6. particularly
g) endangered	7. decaying
h) at the mercy of	8. dreadful
i) growing	9. threatened
j) housing	10. advice
k) crumbling and rotting	11. misuse
l) counselling	12. gain

TIPP

Zahlreiche Faktoren beeinflussen die Art und Weise, wie der Text beim Leser ankommt. Schon bevor man mit dem Lesen beginnt, wirkt das Layout, also die äußere Aufmachung, auf den Leser. Ist der Text ruhig und sachlich gehalten oder schrill und Aufsehen erregend gestaltet? Ebenso schafft die gewählte Sprache eine Atmosphäre (Ton), die den Leser beeinflusst. Wenn z. B. Stimmungen beschrieben werden, verwendet man Adjektive und Adverbien wie sad, optimistic, tragic, positive, romantic. *Versuche deshalb immer zu beantworten, welche Sprache der Autor verwendet und wie sie auf den Leser wirkt. Welches Ziel verfolgt er damit?*

4. *Language: Reread the appeal carefully (Text "Shelter") and write about the* ***effect*** *it has on you. Use examples from the text to support your answer. You should write between 7 and 10 sentences (100 words). Consider the following in your answer: – the title – the language used – the tone of the appeal – the layout of the extract – the purpose of the examples.*

5. *Imagine you want to raise money in school for "Runaway Relief", a charity organisation which provides emergency accommodation for teenage runaways. You are given 3 minutes in which to make an appeal during a special assembly. Parents, teachers and fellow students will attend. Write an appeal of about ten sentences (100–150 words). You may use the ideas in Text A (p. 62–63) to help you.*

TIPP **Einen Aufruf gestalten**

- *Fange mit etwas Einprägsamem an, das die Aufmerksamkeit der Zuhörer oder Leser gewinnt (z. B. einer schockierenden Statistik oder einem Beispiel).*
- *Strukturiere deinen Aufruf durch folgende Fragen: Wer sind wir? Was wollen wir? Warum? Wie kann man uns helfen? (Führe dir deine Zielgruppe vor Augen: Eltern, Lehrer, Gleichaltrige.)*
- *Benutze überzeugende Sprache und Überredungskunst.*

EXTRACT FROM A TRAVEL GUIDE

TIPP

Reiseführer

Sicher hast du schon einmal einen Reiseführer gelesen. Ist dir dabei aufgefallen, dass die meisten Führer gut gegliederte Texte haben, die es dem Reisenden erleichtern, bestimmte Informationen schnell zu finden? Aber auch die Verfasser von Reiseführern haben bestimmte Zielgruppen im Auge. Natürlich passen sie die Sprache entsprechend der Leserschaft an. Der folgende Auszug stammt aus einem Reiseführer für Rucksacktouristen.

SYDNEY, AUSTRALIA

Population: 3,700,000
As Australia's oldest and largest city, Sydney ("Sinney" to the locals) has plenty to offer. Because Sydney grew in a piecemeal fashion, it has a tighter, more congested centre. It's also a dazzlingly modern city, with the most energy and style in Australia.
The stupendous harbour though is more than just the centrepiece for the city, everything in Sydney revolves around it. Would the Opera House, for example, be anything like the place it is, if it wasn't perched right beside the harbour?

City Views
Sydney is becoming a mini-Manhattan and from up top you can look down on the convoluted streets.
Highest is the Sydney Tower on top of the Centrepoint complex on Market St. This gigantic column has a viewing gallery and revolving restaurants on the summit, 305 metres above street level.
The Harbour Bridge is a good vantage point and you can climb the 200 stairs inside for panoramic views of the harbour and city.
Mrs Macquarie's Point, a headland east of the Opera House, has been a lookout since at least 1810 when Elizabeth Macquarie, wife of the governor, had a stone chair hewn into the rock, from where she would watch for ships entering the harbour.

Sydney Opera House
Whether you're at a free Sunday concert or sitting in the open-air restaurant watching the harbour life, the Opera House is a truly memorable place.
It has four auditoriums and puts on dance, theatre, concerts and films as well as opera. Popular performances sell out quickly but there are often 'restricted view' tickets available. There are often free lunch hour concerts and recitals.

Darling Harbour
A small harbour transformed into a major tourist site, Darling is a recreation ground packed with restaurants, shops, as well as many tourist attractions. Among these are the Sydney Aquarium whose all-Australian inhabitants include river fish, Barrier Reef fish, coral gardens, and crocodiles. Two 'oceanarium' tanks, with sharks, rays and other big fish in one, and Sydney Harbour marine life in the other are moored in the harbour. The Powerhouse Museum which covers the decorative arts, science and technology and social history can also be found in Darling Harbour. It's open from 10 am to 5 pm daily and an admission fee is charged (free on the first Saturday of the month).

Art Gallery of New South Wales
The art gallery has an excellent permanent display of Australian, European, Asian and tribal art. There are also temporary exhibits and special exhibitions. Admission is free but fees may apply for the latter (special exhibitions).

Parks
Centennial Park is Sydney's biggest park with running, cycling and horse tracks, duck ponds and barbecue sites.
Balls Head Reserve is located on the north shore of the harbour west of the Harbour Bridge. It is a pocket of bushland with great views of the harbour and old Aboriginal rock paintings and carvings. Some of the other numerous parks in Sydney are Hyde Park, Sydney Olympic Park, and the Royal Botanical Gardens which has a hop-on hop-off trackless train to get around the Gardens' highlights.

Beaches

Sydney's beaches are one of its greatest assets. There are harbour beaches and ocean beaches. Harbour beaches are sheltered and calm and generally smaller; ocean beaches often has good surf. Swimming is considered safe. Shark patrols operate through the summer and ocean beaches are netted to prevent shark attacks. Probably the best known beach in Sydney is Bondi with a selection of cheap accommodation and eating places. Other beaches in and around Sydney include, Watsons Bay, Lady Bay, Tamarama, Manly, Curl Curl, and Narabeen. There's good diving from ocean beaches and shipwrecks to explore from boat dives. Canoeing, kayaking, sailing and of course surfing are popular water sports and readily available to tourists.

Places to Stay

There is a wide selection of accommodation including top range hotels, countless travellers' hostels, bed & breakfasts and camping facilities (generally a long way from town).

Entertainment and Eating Out

Sydney has an enormous range of eateries offering an equally impressive range of cuisines, a reflection of the country's ethnic diversity. For a splurge, consider Kables or Doyle's. Otherwise the selection of mid-range to cheap eating places which offer snacks, main courses or full meals is easy to find.

Simply wandering around the city is entertainment in itself. Last minute tickets for various performances and shows around town can be obtained from Halftix. In addition there are nightclubs with a variety of music to suit most tastes, cinemas and spectator sports – Australians love their 'rugby' and 'cricket'.

(extract taken from Lonely Planet – travel survival kit 1994 edition, ISBN 0-86442-233-4 Lonely Planet Publications: Head Office: PO Box 617, Hawthorn, Vic 3122, Australia)

Vocabulary:

piecemeal – allmählich, schrittweise
perched – platziert, ruhend
convoluted – verschachtelt
vantage point – Aussichtspunkt
headland – Landspitze
hewn [hju:n] – gehauen
moored – festgemacht
splurge – Kauforgie

1. *READING COMPREHENSION – Without reading the text again, complete the following task.*

a) *What is considered Sydney's most magnificent landmark?*

b) *Which other international cityscape is Sydney compared to?*

c) *What is the highest structure in Sydney?*

d) *If you wanted to go out to an expensive restaurant in Sydney, where would you go?*

e) *How did Mrs. Macquarie's point get its name?*

2. *Complete these sentences. Use your own words where possible.*

a) *There is an array of international restaurants in Sydney because ...*

b) *Shark nets are placed at ocean beaches to ...*

c) *It is hard to get tickets for popular performances at the Opera House, but ...*

d) *If you appreciate Aboriginal tribal art, you ...*

e) *Aboriginal rock paintings can ...*

3. *Write a proposed one day itinerary of a trip to Sydney. Use information from the text. You may write in point form.*

FILM REVIEW

ÜBUNGSTIPP

Zum Aufbau und zu den typischen Merkmalen von Rezensionen findest du Infos im Kapitel „Schreiben" auf *S. 46 ff.* *Diese gelten auch für Filmrezensionen.*

1. *Read the following review of the popular film* Bend It Like Beckham.

Bend It Like Beckham

There is only one word to describe this film: fantastic! And the director, Gurinder Chadha, deserves as many awards as she can fit onto her mantelpiece! A teenage coming-of-age comedy, *Bend it like Beckham* is about two 18-year-old London girls with their hearts set on a future in professional soccer. One of them, Jess, is from an Indian family trying to raise their daughter in a traditional way. Unlike her older sister, Pinky, who is preparing for an Indian wedding and a life as a housewife and mother, Jess wants to play soccer like her hero David Beckham. She secretly joins a local women's team. When her parents find out, they forbid her to continue playing, but she keeps sneaking back to the field. Eventually Jess is forced to make a choice between tradition and sport and her family must decide whether to let her follow her dream. Jules, Jess' friend and teammate, is also facing some problems at home. She is always watched by her mother, who is worried that her soccer-loving tomboy daughter is a lesbian.

Bend it like Beckham is a must-see, a real feel-good film of wonderful characters. It is colourful, exciting and absolutely hilarious. Some scenes can really hit home such as mothers always talking about what other people will think and what will give the family a bad reputation. There are also some touching father-daughter moments in both the Asian and the English families.

The only weakness is that the film runs on too long. If the referee had blown her whistle earlier, it would have been absolutely perfect. But since it's the kind of film that will have the whole audience clapping and crying at the end, it is easy to forgive that minor detail.

Vocabulary:
mantelpiece – Kamin
have one's heart set on s.th. – sich auf etwas freuen, erwarten
sneak – schleichen
tomboy – Range, wilder Kerl
hilarious – sehr witzig, urkomisch
hit home – bekannt vorkommen
referee – Schiedsrichter

2. *Reading Comprehension: Answer the questions in your own words.*

a) Why does Jess have to join a soccer team in secret?

b) What would Jess and Jules like to do for a living later on in life?

c) Even if you have not seen the film, why do you think Jules' mother fears her daughter is a lesbian?

TIPP

Bildlicher Wortschatz

Manchmal werden in Ausdrücken Wörter verwendet, bei denen nicht die direkte Bedeutung (literal meaning) entscheidend ist, sondern eine Bedeutung im übertragenen Sinn – also eine dahinter steckende Idee (figurative meaning). Diese kann man aus dem Kontext erschließen.

touching (l.18), unlike (l. 6), facing (l.12), to forgive (l. 22), blown her whistle (l. 20–21), coming of age (l. 4)

3. *Vocabulary: Find words and expressions from the above list similar in meaning to those below.*

a) growing up

b) to be confronted with

c) moving (emotionally)

d) stopped the game

e) to overlook

f) in opposite to

4. *Read the review again and write down examples that show the reviewer's opinion (at least three sentences).*

EXAMPLE *There is only one word to describe this film: fantastic!*

5. *Expansion: Imagine you are Jess trying to make a decision about whether to continue playing soccer against your parents' wishes. Make a list of the reasons for and against. You may do this in note form.*

	Reasons For	**Against**
Playing soccer		

Lyrik

Gedichte solltest du zunächst einfach auf dich wirken lassen, denn sie sind oft sprachliche Kunstwerke. Um ein Gedicht analysieren und interpretieren zu können, solltest du die wichtigsten formalen und sprachlichen Elemente bedenken, über die du zu einer Deutung gelangen kannst.

- *Formaler Aufbau: Strophenaufbau, Reimmuster (z. B.* abab *oder* abba*) und Metrum (= Rhythmus)*
- *Inhaltlicher Aufbau: Überschrift, Thema, Motiv, Atmosphäre, Handlung, lyrisches Ich (Autor)*
- *Sprachliche Gestaltung: Schlüsselwörter, Wortwahl, Stilmittel, Layout, Satzbau, Interpunktion*

1. *Read the poem.*

Robert Hayes: Protest of a Sixth Former

Oh Father can cease to exist
If his nagging must persist.
Respect for parents may be,
But he just drives me crazy
With his craving for a perfect son,
Not this scruffy lout and bum.

Oh mother can live elsewhere,
For me she has only one care:
That of my Sixth Form work
Just so I can be a clerk.
Why can't I go out at nights
Instead of having parental fights?

Oh Gran can go away,
She has nothing useful to say,
Just goes on about her youth
And telling me that I'm uncouth.
Why can't she shut up and draw her pension-
She knows I'm beyond her comprehension.

Vocabulary:
cease – aufhören
craving – brennender Wunsch, Verlangen
scruffy lout – ungepflegter Lümmel
bum – Penner
clerk – Büroangestellter
uncouth – ordinär, vulgär

(Ian Barr and David Bazen: GCSE English Homework Book, London (Letts Educational Publishers) 2000, p. 135)

2. *Form / Language / Style*

a) *Read the poem out loud in the voice of the person who is speaking (poetic voice) What tone of voice do you use and why?*
b) *What does the choice of words tell us about the poet's intention?*
c) *Comment on the rhyming scheme of the poem. Look at the last word of each line and find the pattern. Why do you think the poet has chosen this particular pattern?*

3. *Interpretation:*

a) *How old do you think the speaker of the poem is? Do you think his attitudes towards his elders (parents and grandmother) is typical of that age group? Why or why not? (Use examples from your own personal experiences to support your answer.)*

b) *Compare the wishes of the parents and grandmother and those of the speaker's. Note down your answers in the grid below.*

4. *Personal Response / Creative Writing:*

a) *How do you think the speaker of the poem feels about himself? Find evidence in the poem to support your ideas.*

b) *Imagine you are the sixth former. Write an email to a friend (complaining) about your home life. Write about 100–150 words.*

To	sam12345@yahuu.com
From	sixth.former@hotsnail.com
Date	10 June 2006
Subject	home life

Hi Sam,

How's it going? Right now life at home is sheer hell for me. Man, my father is constantly on my back ...

The diary form is a personal written record of daily events, facts and experiences. It is normally not intended for an audience but for personal use and the tone is generally confessional (secretive) or self-reflective. The entries below are taken from two of Sue Townsend's books written in diary form – here the diary is used as a deliberate literary form.
Adrian Mole is a fictional character. He is a teenager experiencing the usual growing pains of puberty and to worsen matters he belongs to a very dysfunctional family.

Sue Townsend, The Diary of Adrian Mole (1982/1984)

A) Thursday 21st May: Barry Kent duffed me up in the cloakroom today. He hung me on one of the coathooks. He called me ... things too bad to write down. My grandma found out about the menacing (my father didn't want her to know on account of her diabetes). She listened to it all, then she put her hat on, thinned her lips and went out. She was gone one hour and seven minutes; she came in, took off her coat, fluffed her hair out and took 27 pounds from the anti-mugger belt round her waist. She said "He won't bother you again, Adrian, but if he does, let me know." Then she got the tea ready.

B) Tuesday January 13th: My father has gone back to work. Thank God! I don't know how my mother sticks him. Mr. Lucas came in this morning to see if my mother needed any help in the house. He is very kind. Mrs. Lucas was next door cleaning the outside windows. The ladder didn't look very safe. I have written to Malcolm Muggeridge, of the BBC, asking him what to do about being an intellectual. I hope he writes back soon because I'm getting fed up being one on my own. I have written a poem, and it only took me two minutes. Even the famous poets take longer than that. It is called "The Tap", but it isn't really about a tap, it's very deep, and about life and stuff like that ... I showed it to my mother, but she laughed. She isn't very bright. She still hasn't washed my PE shorts, and it is school tomorrow. She is not like the mothers on television.

(Sue Townsend, The Secret Diary of Adrian Mole aged 13¾; The Growing Pains of Adrian Mole, London: Methuen 1982 und 1984)

Vocabulary:
duff up s.o. – jemanden „fertig machen"
menace – drohen
fluff out – *hier:* ordnen
anti-mugger belt – besonders gesicherter Geldgürtel
stick s.o. – jemanden aushalten, ertragen
ladder – Leiter
tap – Wasserhahn
get fed up – etwas Leid sein

1. *Reading Comprehension – Answer in complete sentences*

a) What do you think Adrian's grandma did to stop Barry Kent from bullying Adrian?
b) Who is Barry Kent and what image of him do we have in the entry?
c) Do you think Adrian has many friends? Why or why not (support your answer with evidence from the text)?
d) What kind of language does Adrian use in his diary?
e) How does Adrian view his mother?

2. *You are Adrian. Write your diary entry for either 22nd May or January 14th. Write about 100 words or 7 lines. Remember the following:*

- be consistent with style (Adrian doesn't begin his diary entries with "Dear ...)
- use the language of a 13–14 yr. old
- stay in character

Jostein Gaarder: Sophie's World

Sophie's World *is a novel about the History of Philosophy. Jostein Gaarder was born in Oslo in 1952.* Sophie's World, *the first of his books to be published in English, has been published in 42 languages and has been a bestseller in all of them. Jostein Gaarder lives in Oslo with his family.*

What is Philosophy?

Dear Sophie,

Lots of people have hobbies. Some people collect old coins or foreign stamps, some do needlework, others spend most of their spare time on a particular sport.

A lot of people enjoy reading. But reading tastes differ widely. Some people only read newspapers or comics some like reading novels, while others prefer books on astronomy, wildlife, or technological discoveries.

If I happen to be interested in horses or precious stones, I cannot expect everyone else to share my enthusiasm. If I watch all the sports programs on TV with great pleasure, I must put up with the fact that other people find sports boring.

Is there nothing that interests us all? Is there nothing that concerns everyone – no matter who they are or where they live in the world? Yes, dear Sophie, there are questions that certainly should interest everyone. They are precisely the questions this course is about.

What is the most important thing in life? If we ask someone living on the edge of starvation, the answer is food. If we ask someone dying of cold, the answer is warmth. If we put the same question to someone who feels lonely and isolated, the answer will probably be the company of other people.

But when these basic needs have been satisfied – will there still be something that everybody needs? Philosophers think so. They believe that man cannot live by bread alone. Of course everyone needs food. And everyone needs love and care. But there is something else – apart from that – which everyone needs, and that is to figure out who we are and why we are here.

Being interested in why we are here is not a 'casual' interest like collecting stamps. People who ask such questions are taking part in a debate that has gone on as long as man has lived an this planet. How the universe, the earth, and life came into being is a bigger and more important question than who won the most gold medals in the last Olympics.

(Jostein Gaarder, Sophie's World, published in 1996 by Phoenix, London p. 11,12)

Vocabulary:
novel – Roman
do needlework – Handarbeiten machen
enthusiasm – Begeisterung
put up with – sich abfinden mit
concern – angehen, betreffen
with great pleasure – mit großem Vergnügen
precisely – genau, präzise
be satisfied – zufrieden sein
casual interest – gelegentliches Interesse
take part in a debate – an einer Debatte teilnehmen

ÜBUNGSTIPP

Das Lesen von Texten dient nicht nur der Informationsentnahme. Es hilft dir auch bei der Erweiterung deines Wortschatzes und der Verbesserung deines Ausdrucksvermögens. Lies möglichst viele Originaltexte, auch wenn du nicht jedes Wort verstehst.

1. *Read the following quotes taken from reviews.*

2. *A lot of adjectives and adverbs are used in the reviews. Underline them with different colours. It is not necessary to understand them all.*

TIPP

Adjektive bestimmen Nomen näher: A perfect novel
Adverbien bestimmen Verben und Adjektive: She can write well; *oder:* a perfectly wrong decision

'Sophie's World is set to become a unique popular classic: a wonderfully engaging mystery story that also forms a completely accessible and lucid introduction to philosophy and philosophers' (The Times)

'An extraordinary achievement' (Sunday Times)

'A terrifically entertaining and imaginative story wrapped round its tough, thought-provoking philosophical heart' (Independent on Sunday)

3. *The excerpt from* Sophie's World *contains a lot of information. At the beginning you find ideas about how to spend spare time. Make a word list on the topic Spare Time.*

4. *The author expresses his ideas about basic needs and philosophical questions. Pick them out.*

5. *What kind of text is it?*

6. *How old is the debate on why we are here?*

7. *What is the most important question on earth? Make sentences with the same structure.*

EXAMPLE *If we ask someone living on the edge of starvation, the answer is food.*

a) If we ask someone looking for a new job
b) If we ask someone wanting a baby
c) If we ask someone who has lost his family in a car accident
d) If we ask someone who has won one million in a lottery
e) If we ask someone who has won the presidential election
f) If we ask someone needing a new kidney
g) If we ask someone who loses his temper

Fabeln kennst du bereits seit vielen Jahren aus dem Deutsch- und Fremdsprachenunterricht. Sie gehören zum Kulturgut vieler Völker.
Fabel (lat. fabula *– Erzählung, Rede, Sage) bedeutet kurze Geschichte, mit der eine Moral oder eine Lehre vermittelt wird. Meist treten Tiere sprechend und handelnd wie Menschen auf. Fabeln können in Versen oder in Prosa abgefasst sein.*
Ein berühmter amerikanischer Fabeldichter war James Thurber (1894–1961). Seine zum Teil absurden Ideen erzielen einen humoristischen Effekt. Vielleicht kennst du seine berühmte Version "The Little Girl and the Wolf" des Grimm'schen Märchens „Rotkäppchen". Seine Moral am Ende des verfremdeten Textes erfreut sicher auch viele Frauenrechtlerinnen: It is not easy to fool little girls nowadays as it used to be.

James Thurber: The Owl who was God (1939)

Once upon a starless midnight there was an owl who sat on the branch of an oak tree. Two ground moles tried to slip quietly by, unnoticed. 'You!' said the owl. 'Who?' they quavered, in fear and astonishment, for they could not believe it was possible for anyone to see them in that thick darkness. 'You two!' said the owl. The moles hurried away and told the other creatures of the field and forest that the owl was the greatest and wisest of all animals because he could see in the dark and because he could answer any question. 'I'll see about that', said a secretary bird, and he called on the owl one night when it was again very dark. 'How many claws am I holding up?' said the secretary bird, 'Two', said the owl, and that was right. 'Can you give me another expression for "that is to say" or "namely"?' asked the secretary bird. 'To wit', said the owl. 'Why does a lover call on his love?' asked the secretary bird. 'Tu woo', said the owl.

The secretary bird hastened back to the other creatures and reported that the owl was indeed the greatest and wisest animal in the world because he could see in the dark and because he could answer any question. 'Can he see in the daytime, too?' asked a red fox. 'Yes', echoed a dormouse and a French poodle. 'Can he see in the daytime, too?' All the other creatures laughed loudly at this silly question, and they set upon the red fox and his friends and drove them out of the region. Then they sent a messenger to the owl and asked him to be their leader.

When the owl appeared among the animals it was high noon and the sun was shining brightly. He walked very slowly, which gave him an appearance of great dignity, and he peered about him with large, staring eyes, which gave him an air of tremendous importance. 'He's God!' screamed a Plymouth Rock hen. And the others took up the cry 'He's God!' So they followed him wherever he went and when he began to bump into things they began to bump into things, too. Finally he came to a concrete high-way and he started up the middle of it and all the other creatures followed him. Presently a hawk, who was acting as outrider, observed a truck coming toward them at fifty miles an hour, and he reported to the secretary bird and the secretary bird reported to the owl. 'There's danger ahead', said the secretary bird. 'To wit'? said the owl. The secretary bird told him. 'Aren't you afraid?' he asked. 'Who?' said the owl calmly, for he could not see the truck. 'He's God!' cried all the creatures again, and they were still crying 'He's God!' when the truck hit them and ran them down. Some of the animals were merely injured, but most of them, including the owl, were killed. Moral: You can fool too many people too much of the time.

(The Thurber Carnival, London: Penguin 1981)

Vocabulary:
ground mole – Maulwurf
slip by – sich davon schleichen
quaver – mit zitternder Stimme sagen
see about sth. – sich kümmern um
secretary bird – Sekretärgeier
claws – Klaue, Kralle
call on – ansprechen
wit – *hier:* Witz, Esprit
woo – umwerben
dormouse – Schlafmaus, Haselmaus
set upon – angreifen
messenger – Boote
high noon – Mittag
dignity – Würde
peer – angestrengt schauen, spähen
air – Ausstrahlung, Aura
Plymouth Rock hen – amerikanische Hühnerzüchtung
bump into – etwas rammen, zusammenstoßen
presently – gegenwärtig, derzeit
hawk – Habicht
outrider – Kundschafter

1. *Read the text again and find out who said these sentences.*

a) 'To wit', said

b) 'How many claws am I holding up?' said.

c) 'He's God', cried .

d) 'He's God', screamed .

e) 'Aren't you afraid?' asked.

f) 'Can he see in the daytime, too?' asked .

2. *What did the animals say about the owl?*

EXAMPLE *The moles hurried away and told the other creatures of the field and forest that the owl was the greatest and wisest of all animals because he could see in the dark and because he could answer any question.*

3. *In fables animals, plants or objects can be the main characters. Underline the direct speech of the characters to make clear who is who. Use different colours.*

4. *What kind of voices could the animals have?*

EXAMPLE *The owl could have a deep and serious voice.*

The moles	The red fox
The secretary bird	A French poodle
The dormouse	The Plymouth Rock hen
A hawk	All the creatures

TIPP

Die Stimme mit ihrem Klang sagt viel über eine Person aus. Sie charakterisiert indirekt. Im Englischen werden dafür die Begriffe indirect *oder* implicit *verwendet.*

5. *Reading Comprehension*

a) Why are the two ground moles so impressed?

b) Why did the secretary bird decide to test the owl?

c) What was the result of the test?

d) Why were the fox and his friends driven out?

e) Why could the owl convince the other animals that he was God?

f) What was the danger for the animals?

g) How did the owl react when he knew a truck was coming?

h) What sex are the owl, the secretary bird, the fox, the dormouse? Give evidence from the text.

i) What happened on the highway?

6. *Retell the story. Use the questions above to help you.*

7. *The red fox was driven out of the region because of his critical question "Can he see in the daytime, too?" What could the creatures have shouted to force him to go away?*

EXAMPLE *They shout, "He is so wise, how can you ask such silly questions."*

8. *No doubt you have realized that this is a fable about dependence and blind obedience. What do you think of obedience?*

9. *Make a list of people you obey blindly. Say why.*

TIPP

Einige Vokabeln zum Wortfeld „laut reden":

English	***German***
to bellow	*brüllen*
to call	*schreien, rufen*
to cry against	*heftig protestieren*
to roar	*brüllen, anbrüllen*
to scream	*schreien, kreischen*
to raise one's voice	*die Stimme erheben*
to holler (informal, AE)	*brüllen*
to yell	*schreien, brüllen*

Urban legends *sind Geschichten von zweifelhafter Glaubwürdigkeit und sagenhaftem Inhalt. Sie drücken Ideen, Gefühle, Befürchtungen, Sorgen und Nöte aus. Sie sind meist mündlich überliefert und unterliegen somit einer ständigen Veränderung.*
Synonyme für urban legends *sind* contemporary legends, urban myth, *im Deutschen etwa „moderne Großstadtsage".*

The Perfect Mousse

A young housewife was to give her first dinner party and her husband had invited several directors from his firm. As it was to be a special dinner, one of the things she intended to prepare was a salmon mousse. With this in mind, she went to the local market, purchased the necessary fish and, after cleaning it, left it on the kitchen table while she gathered up the rest of the ingredients. Returning from the larder, to her horror, she found the cat sitting on the table chewing the fish. She chased the cat away and thought – "Well, it is not as if they will know that the cat has nibbled on the fish." Accordingly she washed and cleaned it again and got on with her preparations.

The dinner party was a great success and, as the evening came to a close, the guests went off into the night making many complimentary comments, particularly about the salmon mousse. Closing the gates after the last car had left, the couple suddenly noticed, by the side of the house porch, their cat very stiff and very dead. Racking her brains, the young housewife tried to think what could have happened to the poor animal, when she remembered the salmon. Thinking the fish must have been contaminated, in desperation she grabbed the phone and called all the dinner guests, including her husband's directors, to explain and advise them to contact their doctors immediately. They were not amused and, in fact, several of the guests were very upset even to think that she had given them food the cat had chewed.

Just as she had made the last call the door-bell rang and there stood their next-door neighbour looking very sheepish. He explained that earlier in the evening he had unfortunately run over their cat in his drive. He was very sorry but he had been in a desperate hurry at the time as he was on his way to meet a train. He had rung the door-bell several times in order to tell them of the accident but, unfortunately, he could not make anyone hear above the noise of the dinner party. Instead, he had left the cat by the porch – had they found it yet?

(Heike Jüngst (Hg.), Urban Legends, Stuttgart: Reclam 1999, p. 32 f.)

Vocabulary:
mousse – Schaumspeise, Mousse
salmon – Lachs
larder – Speisekammer
chew – kauen
chase away – wegjagen
nibble – knabbern
get on with s.th. – weitermachen
come to a close – sich dem Ende zuneigen
complimentary – lobend, anerkennend
porch – Eingangsbereich, Veranda
contaminated – vergiftet
in desperation – verzweifelt
sheepish – beschämt, verlegen

1. *Read and enjoy the urban legend.*

URBAN LEGEND

2. *Read the urban legend again and find the correct order according to the text.*

a) The guests made complimentary comments about the salmon mousse.
b) The neighbour explained he had unfortunately run over the cat.
c) She went to the supermarket and bought the fish.
d) The dinner party was a great success.
e) She believed the fish was contaminated and called all guests to explain and advise them to contact their doctors.
f) A young wife had to give her first dinner party.
g) Her cat was sitting on the kitchen table and was chewing the fish.
h Very important guests were invited by her husband.
i) Their guests were not amused.
j) She cleaned the fish.
k) She left the kitchen for a moment.
l) She thought about the reasons for the cat's death.
m) She washed and cleaned the fish again and got on with preparations.
n) After saying goodbye to the guests the couple noticed their cat was dead.
o) The neighbour was very sorry but he could not apologise earlier because he was in a hurry and nobody heard the doorbell rang.
p) He had left the cat by the porch.
q) She intended to prepare a salmon mousse.

3. *The young couple had an argument about the evening. Write a dialogue.*

4. *It is the next day in the husband's company. How does his boss handle the situation?*

5. *There are many sentences with participles in the original text. Underline the participles.*

EXAMPLE *Returning from the larder, to her horror, she found the cat sitting on the table chewing the fish.*

TIPP

Partizipialkonstruktionen können im Deutschen gut als Nebensätze wiedergegeben werden. Beispiel: Als sie aus der Speisekammer kam, fand sie zu ihrem Entsetzen die Katze, wie sie auf dem Tisch saß und den Fisch anknabberte.

6. *The young wife calls all the guests to warn them because she fears the fish was contaminated. Read the fragments of the phone call and fill in the gaps.*

A: the young wife

B: a person in the boss's house

A: Hello, this is Mary Miller. Could I speak to Richard Taylor, please?

B: Hold on a moment, please.

A: OK, thank you.

B: I'm afraid Mr Taylor is not ____________________.

A: Oh, I see. Have you got any idea when ____________________?

B: No, ____________________. Can I give ____________________?

A: No, it is impossible. I must speak to him now.

B: Could he ____________________?

A: Oh, sorry but I have to warn Mr Taylor. You know he was a guest at our dinner party and something rather unfortunate happened. ____________________.

7. *Now retell the story in your own words.*

TIPP

Beim Nacherzählen verwendet man Zeitformen der Vergangenheit. Es kommt auch auf einen guten Stil an, der sich durch gute Übergänge zwischen den Sätzen auszeichnet. Folgende Wendungen können dir dabei helfen, Gedanken und Argumente in eine gute Reihenfolge zu bringen:
First, ... / Secondly ...., /..., but ... / Another important point is ... / Also ... / Finally ... / and ..., because ... On the other hand ... / a different aspect is ... / ...
Folgende Konjunktionen und Präpositionen dienen dazu, Sätze und Satzteile logisch und zeitlich miteinander zu verknüpfen: ... and / but / because ...; Then ...; After that ...; Although / however ...; If ...

TEST: LESEN

Gary Younge (New York): NYPD moves to a new beat

In New York, the home of hip-hop, rap is a serious business. This is the city that is home to the place (Sugar Hill, Harlem) that produced the group (the Sugar Hill Gang) that gave us the record (Rapper's Delight) that made rap mainstream. Rap has risen beyond the status of a music genre to the level of a viable modern state. New York is the capital of the hip-hop "nation", which is ruled by the hip-hip "generation", whose turf wars are resolved at hip-hop "summits", during which the hip-hop "community" get together to promote and protect hip-hop "culture". Professor Todd Boyd, a hip-hop "academic", argues: "You might get a better read of what's going on in the world of black people today by listening to DMX on It's Dark and Hell Is Hot than by listening to repeated broadcasts of Martin Luther King speeches."

This state has got its own police force. The New York Police Department has assigned a team of detectives to patrol the hip-hop nation – studying songs, scrutinizing artistic battles, visiting clubs and monitoring business feuds. Last November Lieutenant Brian Burke told the New York Times that following the murder of Jam Master Jay, the DJ for Run-DMC, the team was looking for leads in the lyrics and criminal connections in the world of rap.

When not covering specific cases, the team of six officers acts as police liaisons with both the hip-hop world and detectives covering a similar beat in California and Florida. Rappers are rarely found alone, preferring instead to travel in "crews", and the detectives keep track of these entourages, going on alert when two sets of rivals are in town at the same time.

Wary of accusations of racial profiling in a city where four African-Americans were shot by police in the first two days of the year, the NYPD is eager to point out that this is not a unit dedicated to hip-hop. "We have a team, within the intelligence unit, that monitors the music industry," said a spokesman. "They deal with the music industry as a whole."

Rap does not simply reflect the faults of American society, it also impacts on them and, all too often, compounds them. Nowhere is this more readily acknowledged than within the hip-hop community itself, which has a vocal reformist wing. Public Enemy's Chuck D is constantly calling on rappers to live up to their potential rather than down to expectations. "Hip-hop has got to look itself in the mirror. It is fomenting too much negativity out here," he says.

It is precisely for this reason that so many African-American politicians and civil rights leaders are so keen to engage with the hip-hop community. They understand what so many of rap's critics refuse to acknowledge – that its power to influence could be harnessed to great, positive effect.

(The Guardian Weekly 20-03-03, page 18)

Vocabulary:
viable – lebensfähig
summit – Gipfeltreffen
patrol – kontrollieren
scrutinize – genau untersuchen
liaison – Verbindung; *hier:* Verbindungsmänner
alert – wachsam, vorsichtig
racial profiling – zu rassistischen Vorurteilen neigend
impact – (stark) beeinflussen
compound – *hier:* schlechten Einfluss ausüben
foment – aufwiegeln, anstacheln
be harnessed – umgeleitet, kanalisiert werden

TEST: LESEN

1. *Reading Comprehension: Read the passage again and answer the questions in complete sentences.*

a) What does the reporter mean when he refers to Rap as a 'viable modern state'?
b) Why do NYPD detectives patrol the hip hop "nation"?
c) How does rap music 'impact on and compound the faults of American society'?
d) Why does "hip-hop" have to look itself in the mirror?

2. *Grammar and Vocabulary: Look at how the underlined words and expressions are used in context and choose the most appropriate meaning from the list below.*

1. ... that made rap mainstream
2. ... whose turf wars are resolved at hip-hop "summits"
3. ... "You might get a better read of what's going on in the world
4. ... the team was looking for leads in the lyrics
5. ... and the detectives keep track of these entourages
6. ... wary of the accusations
7. ... it is fomenting too much negativity
8. ... leaders are so keen to engage with the hip-hop
9. ... critics refuse to acknowledge
10. ... its power to influence could be harnessed to

Yo, I was schooled by the hood,
raised by the wolves –
Trained by the pain,
adopted by guerrillas –
Got tattoos wit' skin and scars from brawls

1.	a) popular	b) the most important pond	c) famous
2.	a) lawn	b) territorial	c) strange
3.	a) book	b) idea	c) understanding
4.	a) clues	b) followers	c) names
5.	a) employ	b) notice	c) keep an eye on
6.	a) afraid	b) cautious	c) ignorant
7.	a) preventing	b) stirring up	c) dreading
8.	a) ready to	b) eager to	c) discouraged to
9.	a) know	b) find out	c) admit
10.	a) channeled	b) strengthend	c) ridden

3. *Read the passage again and decide if the statements are true or not.*

a) Hip-hop was invented in Los Angeles.
b) NYPD is a New York rap group.
c) Professor Todd Boyd researches rap and hip hop culture.
d) The police tried to find clues in the lyrics of rap music after DJ M Jay was murdered.
e) Most black musicians and citizens trust the police department wholeheartedly.
f) Chuck Dee wants rap music to have a positive influence on his listeners.
g) American politicians refuse to associate with the hip hop community.
h) Rap's critics agree with what Chuck Dee claims.

4. *Personal Response: Do you think popular music, such as rap music, has a responsibility to present positive messages for today's youth? Feel free to use examples from popular songs or raps you know to support your answer. Write about 150 words.*

Allgemeine Hinweise zum Schreiben

- Lies die Aufgabenstellung zum Schreiben immer genau (wenn notwendig auch mehrmals) durch und achte auf die geforderte Umsetzung.
- Wähle eine Stilebene, die der Aufgabenstellung angemessen ist.
- Überlege dir, welche Zeitform du verwenden musst. Häufig geht dies aus der Fragestellung oder der Art der Aufgabe hervor.
- Wechsle nicht zwischen verschiedenen Varianten des Englischen, entscheide dich entweder für das britische oder das amerikanische Englisch.
- Beginne die Umsetzung der Aufgabenstellung mit einer Mindmap oder Stichpunkten, in denen du Ideen für deinen Text sammelst und sortierst, bevor du mit dem eigentlichen Schreiben des Textes beginnst.
- Gliedere deinen Text in Sinneinheiten.
- Nimm dir immer ausreichend Zeit zum Kontrolllesen und für die Korrektur. Das schließt auch ein, dass du überprüfst, ob du die Aufgabenstellung vollständig und richtig erfüllt hast.

Writing an email

To	robin.peterson@yahuu.com
From	miriam.roberts@hotsnail.com
Date	13 January 2006
Subject	Your party

Hi Robin

Thanks for the invitation to your party. Of course, I'll come!
See you later.

Miriam

Schreiben einer E-Mail

- Eine E-Mail ist meist knapp und treffend formuliert.
- Der Stil kann informell sein. Auf keinen Fall sollte man zwischen verschieden Stilebenen wechseln.
- Anrede und Briefabschluss können einfach und kurz sein, sollten aber nicht weggelassen werden.
- Anrede und Namen trennt man vom eigentlichen Brief/Hauptteil durch je eine Leerzeile.
- Die Betreffzeile *(subject)* sollte aussagekräftig sein und nicht vergessen werden.

1. *Write an email to a friend inviting him or her to your birthday party. (Tell him/her when the party begins, where it is and what to bring.)*

a) Informal letters

Absender kann hier weggelassen werden	
Schreibweise des Datums beachten (ohne Punkt)	6 January 2006
Dear + Vornamen als Anrede	Dear Aunt Sarah,
	I'd like to thank you for the fantastic holiday I spent at your house and for your kind hospitality. I'll always remember my first stay with you. Thanks for the wonderful excursions you organised for the two of us. It gave me a chance to see a lot of your beautiful country and especially the area with all those
Gebrauch des informellen *I'm, you're* an Stelle von *I am, we are* möglich	marvellous lakes and forests. I'm sending the best photos I took as a souvenir of my stay. I'll never forget the great evening we spent with your neighbours. What a barbecue! I think we all enjoyed it a lot. Thanks again for your generosity. I'm looking forward to seeing you here in June to show
Briefabschlüsse: *Love, Love from; Lots of love* für enge Freunde, sonst auch *All the best, Take care, See you soon, Best wishes (to you all), Regards*	you a little of my country in return. All the best, Nancy

1. *Write a thank-you letter to your grandma in which you say thank you for the wonderful birthday present she gave you – money for a trip you want to go on together with a friend.*

b) Formal letters – Letter of application

Schreibweise des Datums beachten (ohne Punkte), Datum rechts oder links	48 Dodsworth Avenue York YO31 8UF 16 February 2006	Absender ohne Namen
Angabe der vollständigen Adresse des Empfängers	Mr Oliver Johnson Personnel Department 6 Exeter Road London NW4 6AB	
Dear + Sir/Madam, wenn Name unbekannt, ansonsten *Dear Mr/Ms/Mrs + Nachnamen*	Dear Mr Johnson, I am writing to apply for the position of assistant hotel manager advertised in the Evening Standard of 11 February. Please find enclosed a copy of my CV.	anstelle von *position* können auch *post* oder *vacancy* verwendet werden
Gliederung formelles Englisch *I am, we are* besser als *I'm, we're*	Since graduating from Cardiff University, I have been working for the *Swan Hotel* in York. I have become particularly interested in welcoming people and caring for their needs and wish to develop my career in that direction.	
Mögliche Briefabschlüsse: Im BE *Yours sincerely,* wenn man den Adressaten mit Namen angesprochen hat, sonst *Yours faithfully*	I would welcome the chance to work in a small dynamic team where I could make a significant contribution while developing my professional skills further. I am available for an interview next week and look forward to hearing from you soon.	
Namen vollständig ausschreiben und darüber eigenhändig unterschreiben	Yours sincerely *Miriam Roberts* Miriam Roberts Enc. CV	Verweis auf Lebenslauf als Anlage

TIPP

Writing a letter of application

Inhaltlich muss die Bewerbung mindestens folgende Bestandteile enthalten:

1. *Angabe, für welchen Job du dich bewirbst und wie du davon erfahren hast*
2. *kurze Beschreibung deiner wichtigsten Qualifikationen bzw. Erfahrungen auf diesem Gebiet*
3. *Erläuterung, warum du den Job haben möchtest und warum du dich dafür geeignet hältst*
4. *Angabe, wie man dich erreicht bzw. wann du für Gespräche zur Verfügung stehst*

Curriculum Vitae

Name	Miriam Roberts
Address	...
Telephone	0288 872790
Mobile	0772 7845673
Email	miriam.roberts@hotsnail.com
Nationality	British
Date of birth	17 June 1982
Place of birth	London
Education	
2000–2003	Aberdeen University: BA in Hotel Trade and Management
1992–1999	Wellington School, 3 A levels: English (A), French (A), Art (B), 8 GCSEs
Employment	
2003–present	*Swan Hotel* York
Skills	Computer literate: familiar with MS Office Fluent French and Spanish Clean driving licence
Hobbies and Interests	Travelling, photography and cooking

References available on request

1. *Write a letter of application for a job you would like to apply for. Using the given example include the necessary items* (Absender, Datum, Adresse, Anrede, Bewerbung, Briefabschluss, Unterschrift und Namen, Hinweis auf Anlage)

2. *Write your CV using the given example. For this you can copy the left column of the table but don't forget to change the details about your education and employment.*

ACHTUNG

Writing your CV

Da sich das deutsche Schulsystem von dem britischen unterscheidet, sollte man die deutschen Bezeichnungen für Schule und Schulabschlüsse in die Bewerbung schreiben und die englischen Entsprechungen dafür (in Klammern oder kursiv) angeben.

Education

2002–2006	Universität Rostock *(Rostock University)* Subjects: English and German
1993–2002	Gymnasium Carolinum Neustrelitz *(grammar school)* Abitur *(A-levels)*
1989–1993	Grundschule *(primary school)*

Als englische Entsprechung für den Realschulabschluss kann *O-levels* angegeben werden.

Isaac Asimov: The fun they had

Margie even wrote about it that night in her diary. On the page headed May 17, 2157, she wrote, "Today Tommy found a real book!"
It was a very old book. Margie's grandfather once said that when he was a little boy his grandfather told him that there was a time when all stories were printed on paper. They turned the pages, which were yellow and crinkly, and it was awfully funny to read words that stood still instead of moving the way they were supposed to – on a screen, you know. And then, when they turned back to the page before, it had the same words on it that it had had when they read it the first time.
"Gee", said Tommy, "what a waste. When you are through with the book, you must throw it away, I guess. Our television screen must have had a million books on it and it's good for plenty more. I wouldn't throw it away."
"Same with mine", said Margie. She was eleven and hadn't seen as many textbooks as Tommy had. He was thirteen.
She said, "Where did you find it?"
"In my house." He pointed without looking, because he was busy reading. "In the attic."
"What's it about?"
"School."
Margie was scornful. "School? What's there to write about school? I hate school."
Margie always hated school, but now she hated it more than ever. The mechanical teacher had been giving her test after test in geography and she had been doing worse and worse until her mother had shaken her head sorrowfully and sent for the County Inspector. ...
She said to Tommy, "Why would anyone write about school?"
Tommy looked at her with very superior eyes. "Because it's not our kind of school, stupid. This is the old kind of school that they had hundred of years ago." He added loftily, pronouncing the word carefully, "*Centuries* ago."
Margie was hurt. "Well, I don't know what kind of school they had all that time ago."

She read the book over his shoulder for a while, then said, “Anyway, they had a teacher.” “Sure they had a teacher, but it wasn’t a *regular* teacher. It was a man.”
“A man? How could a man be a teacher?”
“Well, he just told the boys and girls things and gave them homework and asked them questions.” “A man isn’t smart enough.”
“Sure he is. My father knows as much as my teacher.”
“He can’t. A man can't know as much as a teacher.”
“He knows almost as much, I betcha.”
Margie wasn’t prepared to dispute that. She said, “I wouldn’t want a strange man in my house to teach me.”
Tommy screamed with laughter. “You don’t know much, Margie. The teacher didn’t live in the house. They had a special building and all the kids went there.”
“And all the kids learnt the same thing?”
“Sure, if they were the same age.”
“But my mother says a teacher has to be adjusted to fit the mind of each boy and girl it teaches and that each kid has to be taught differently.”
“Just the same they didn’t do it that way then. If you don’t like it, you don’t have to read the book.”
“I didn’t say I didn’t like it,” Margie said quickly. She wanted to read about those funny schools. They weren’t even half finished when Margie’s mother called, “Margie! School!”
Margie looked up. “Not yet, Mamma.”
“Now!” said Mrs. Jones. “And it’s probably time for Tommy, too.”
Margie said to Tommy, “Can I read the book some more with you after school?”
“Maybe,” he said nonchalantly. He walked away whistling, the dusty old book tucked beneath his arm. Margie went into the schoolroom. It was right next to her bedroom, and the mechanical teacher was on and waiting for her. It was always on at the same time every day except Saturday and Sunday, because her mother said little girls learned better if they learned at regular hours.
The screen was lit up, and it said: “Today’s arithmetic lesson is on the addition of proper fractions. Please insert yesterday’s homework in the proper slot.”
Margie did so with a sigh. She was thinking about the old schools they had when her grandfather’s grandfather was a little boy. All the kids from the whole neighborhood came, laughing, and shouting in the schoolyard, sitting together in the schoolroom, going home together at the end of the day. They learned the same things, so they could help one another on the homework and talk about it. And the teachers were people ...
The mechanical teacher was flashing on the screen: “When we add the fractions 1/2 and 1/4 ...” Margie was thinking about how the kids must have loved it in the old days. She was thinking about the fun they had.

(Isaac Asimov: Earth is Room Enough (New York: Doubleday & Co Inc., 1957), pp. 134 ff., in: Previews, Langenscheidt-Longman 1995, S. 95 f.)

Vocabulary:

headed – datiert
crinkly – zerknittert
plenty more – noch viel mehr
attic – Dachboden
sorrowfully – betrübt
County Inspector – Bezirksschulrat
loftily – stolz
I betcha – wette ich
dispute – sich über etwas streiten
laughter – Lachen
adjusted to fit the mind – *hier:* dem geistigen Vermögen angepasst
nonchalantly – gleichgültig
tucked beneath his arm – unter seinem Arm
at regular hours – immer zur gleichen Zeit / regelmäßig
proper fractions – echte Brüche
insert something in the proper slot – etwas in den richtigen Schlitz tun
sigh – Seufzer
flash – aufleuchten

Writing a summary

- Eine Zusammenfassung enthält das Wesentliche eines Textes.
- Sie gibt Antwort auf die fünf Fragen *who, where, when, what, why.*
- Eine Zusammenfassung sollte im *simple present* und mit eigenen Worten verfasst werden.
- Sie enthält weder Beispiele noch andere Einzelheiten.
- In einer Zusammenfassung wird keine direkte Rede verwendet.
- Sie darf keine eigene Meinung oder Interpretation enthalten.

Vorgehensweise:

- Lies den Text und schlage die unbekannten Wörter nach, die für das Textverständnis notwendig sind.
- Markiere wichtige Aussagen, insbesondere die Stellen, die Antwort auf die Fragen: *wer, wo, wann, was* und *warum* geben.
- Mache dir Notizen zur Beantwortung der fünf Fragen.
- Achte beim Schreiben der Zusammenfassung darauf, dass du durchgängig *simple present* verwendest, selbst wenn der Originaltext im *past* steht. Wechsle auf keinen Fall zwischen *present* und *past*.
- Sollte für die Zusammenfassung eine Wortzahl vorgegeben sein, musst du sie einhalten und darfst weder wesentlich mehr noch weniger schreiben. Notfalls gehe deine Zusammenfassung noch einmal durch und streiche weniger wichtige Fakten. Auch durch die Sprache kannst du die Wortzahl verringern, z. B. durch den Gebrauch von Partizipien anstelle von Relativsätzen.
- Zum Schluss überprüfe, ob du alle fünf Fragen beantwortet hast.
- Wenn du mit dem Inhalt deiner Zusammenfassung zufrieden bist, achte auch auf deinen Ausdruck und die sprachliche Richtigkeit.

1. *Write a summary of* "The fun they had" *in about 100 words. First of all answer shortly the five WH-questions (where, when, who, what, why) in order to structure your summary.*

TIPP

Die englische Entsprechung für die Geschichte spielt ... *ist:* the story is set (in)... *oder:* the action takes places (in)... *für* die Handlung spielt ...

How to write a diary entry

Bei einem Tagebucheintrag gibst du meistens nicht nur die Fakten eines Ereignisses oder Tages wieder, sondern du reflektierst auch über die Geschehnisse, d. h. du bringst deine Gedanken und Empfindungen dazu zum Ausdruck.
Oft schreiben Menschen, die ein Tagebuch führen, über Geheimnisse oder über Gefühle, Hoffnungen und Wünsche, die sie für sich allein behalten wollen.
Wenn du also die Aufgabe erhältst, anstelle einer anderen Person einen „Tagebucheintrag" zu schreiben, musst du versuchen, so viel wie möglich über diese Person zu erfahren, um dich mit ihr identifizieren zu können. Z. B. muss die Sprache der Herkunft und dem Alter der Person entsprechen. Solche Informationen musst du dem Text entnehmen, der als Grundlage für die Aufgabenstellung dient. Handelt es sich um einen Jugendlichen, ist es völlig gerechtfertigt, auch Umgangssprache zu verwenden.
Vergiss nicht, den Tagebucheintrag in geeigneter Form zu beginnen (z. B. Dear diary, ...) und abzuschließen (Yours, Name des Tagebuchführers) sowie die Datumsangabe.

ÜBUNGSTIPP

Vorgehensweise

Markiere vor dem Schreiben des Tagebucheintrags alle Textstellen, die dir helfen, dich mit Margie zu identifizieren. Versuche zu verstehen, warum was passiert. Sammle Informationen über Margie, ihr Verhältnis zu anderen und darüber, wie ihre Umwelt sie wahrnimmt, aber auch über Dinge, die an diesem Tag und im Vorfeld geschehen sind.

1. *Write Margie's diary entry for the day she read the book for the first time (200–250 words). Start for example like this:*

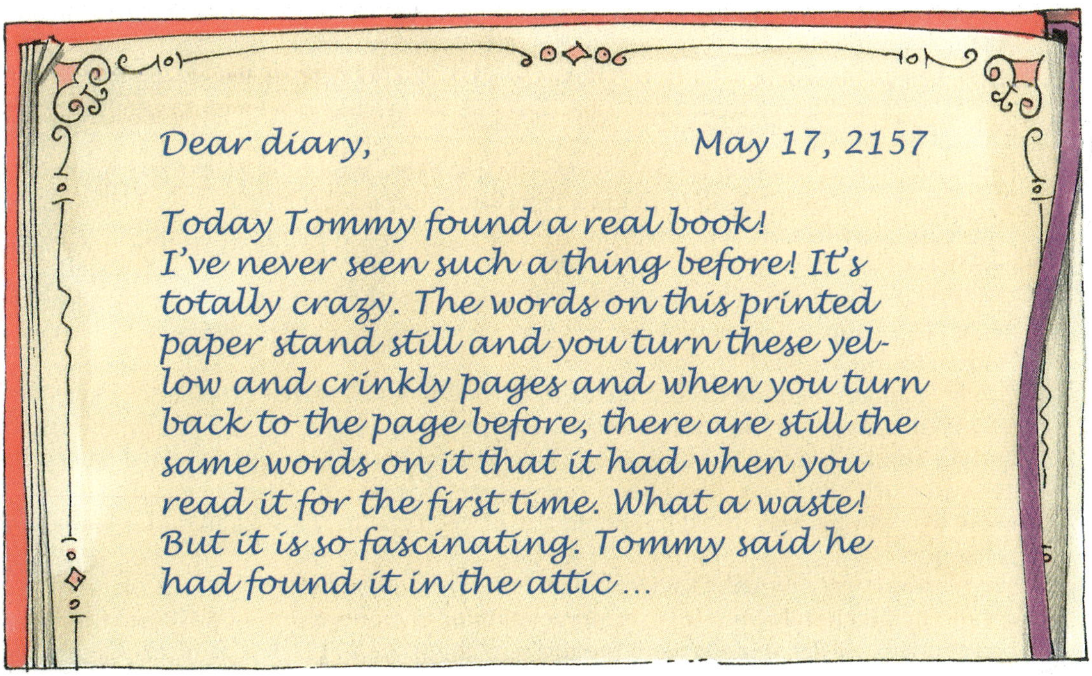

Toeckey Jones: The Meeting (1979)

Toeckey Jones was born and grew up in South Africa, but in 1971 moved to London where he now lives and works as a full-time writer. His first novel, *Go Well, Stay Well*, was published in 1979, and was welcomed as one of the few novels for young readers to describe what it is like to grow up in a racially segregated society.

Candice was a 17-year-old white South African girl from Johannesburg. One day, while walking in the city, she tripped and twisted her ankle.

Almost immediately she felt a gentle touch on her arm. She opened her eyes to see a young African girl standing in front of her. Instinctively, Candy's grip on her bag tightened. The girl could be after her money. Candy knew how clever the young black pickpockets in the city were said to be. She was always being warned to keep a close hold on her purse.

"You OK?" Without waiting for an answer, the girl bent down to inspect Candy's ankle. "Tch ... tch ... shame." Shaking her head she straightened up.

"That's no good to walk on," she said. "You can sit down in the park. It's not far. Come, I must help you."

The girl took hold of Candy's free arm and after a moment's hesitation, Candy allowed herself to be supported as they began to move slowly along the pavement.

"Too many drinks, hey?" the girl teased.

Candy laughed, then felt herself blushing as she became aware of the curious stares they were attracting. She tried to move faster, leaning as little as possible on the supporting arm beside her. She still wasn't sure she could trust the girl. It would have been so much simpler if it had been a white person who had offered help. She didn't know why the girl was doing it. Should she offer to pay her? It was all rather embarrassing.

The park was only two blocks away, but it seemed an age before they got there. As the girl helped her down into a sitting position on the grass, Candy was aware of her bag slipping off her shoulder and the girl stretching out to catch it as it fell. Candy

held her breath, her heart beating fast. But the girl didn't run off. Instead, she waited until Candy was sitting comfortably, and then handed the bag to her.
"Better now?" she asked.
While the girl bent down to take a closer look at the injured ankle, Candy studied her thoughtfully. She was really rather pretty, Candy discovered to her surprise, for she had never thought of African features as being attractive before. But this girl's features were all in perfect proportion to each other giving her face as a whole an open, sunny expression.
Candy didn't want her to go. She had never met an African girl of her own age before – at least not to speak to. And she was already beginning to like this girl who seemed undecided about her next move and was playing nervously with the worn collar of her blouse, trying to do up a button that wasn't there.
"Are you in hurry?" Candy asked.
"No, Why? Can I give you a lift home? My Mercedes is just round the corner."
Candy laughed and the girl sat down on the grass beside her.
"What's your name?" she asked.
"Candice. But everyone calls me Candy. And yours?"
"Rebecca. But everyone calls me Becky." And then they both laughed. "Tell you what." Candy said. "I'm thirsty. How about you?"
"Sure. What would you like? I'll go and get it. Beer?"
"I think I'd better have a Coke. But let's go and sit down somewhere, and perhaps have something to eat as well. So long as I don't have to walk too far, my ankle should be all right."
"You know a place we can go?" Becky asked.
Candy's face slowly reddened with embarrassment. For a moment she had completely forgotten. There wasn't anywhere they could go together. Within ten minutes' walk of where they were sitting, there were at least three restaurants or coffee bars. But Becky couldn't go into them – they were all exclusively for whites. Further away there were a few cafés for African workers travelling daily into Johannesburg from the black township of Soweto. But even if Candy could have walked that far with her bad ankle, she would be stopped from going into any of them with Becky.
"Do you want us to get arrested?" Becky teased.

The two girls continue to talk for some time and agree to meet again. Candy then telephones her father and asks him to come and fetch her.

Candy caught sight of a blue Cortina and identified her father at the wheel.
"My dad's here," she said unnecessarily, for Becky had already got to her feet and was quickly brushing the grass off her skirt.
"I must go," she told Candy.
"Wait ... Hold on, we haven't settled anything. We don't even know how to get in touch with each other."
Candy wasn't really surprised that Becky wanted to get away before her father arrived, but she wanted the two of them to meet. It would make it easier to talk about Becky to her father later.
Suddenly Candy's father came up behind them.
"What have you done to yourself?" he called out to Candy. Becky turned round and immediately stepped aside, separating herself from the other two.
"Hello, Dad," Candy said. "Dad, this is Becky," she went on quickly. "She's been helping me and looking after me."

"Oh." He turned and glanced at Becky, who bowed her head shyly.

"Good afternoon, sir," she said politely.

"Uh ... hello." He was already bending down to look at Candy's ankle.

"Is it very painful?" he asked.

Candy shook her head impatiently. She was aware that Becky had moved a little further away and was fidgeting nervously.

"Dad!" Candy said firmly. "Becky has been absolutely marvellous. I don't know what I would have done without her."

"Oh." He smiled briefly in Becky's direction. "That was very kind of her. Now, do you think you'll be able to walk as far as the car?"

Candy was disappointed. He could at least show some interest in Becky, and talk to her directly. She pulled a face at him, and glanced at Becky.

"What?... Oh, yes, of course."

Too late. Candy realised that he had misunderstood her. Putting his hand into his pocket, he said, "Here, this is for being so kind and looking after my daughter until I got here," and he held a one rand note out to her.

Helplessly, Candy stared at them both, red with shame. Anything she said now could only make the situation worse. She felt furious with her father, but she knew she couldn't really blame him for misunderstanding her. One glance at Becky was enough to see how poor she was. And normally white people automatically tipped Africans for any help they gave. But after everything that had passed between her and Becky, offering Becky money could only seem an insult.

Candy couldn't bear to watch but she had to. She saw Becky look up and slowly begin to shake her head.

(Toeckey Jones: "The Meeting", from *Go Well, Stay Well,* © The Bodley Head, London 1979; in: *Step up,* Diesterweg 1991)

Vocabulary:
racially segregated society – auf Rassentrennung basierende Gesellschaft
trip – stolpern
twist one's ankle – sich den Fußknöchel verstauchen
grip – Griff
hesitation – Zögern
tease – necken, hänseln
blush – erröten
embarrassing – peinlich
injure – verletzen
worn collar – verschlissener Kragen
redden – erröten
exclusively – ausschließlich
arrest – verhaften
settle – sich einigen, entscheiden
bow – sich verbeugen
fidget – mit etwas herumspielen
marvellous – wunderbar
rand note – in Südafrika verwendeter Geldschein
furious – wütend
blame – Schuld
glance – Blick
tip – jdm. Trinkgeld geben
insult – Beleidigung
bear – ertragen

1. *Write a summary of the story "The Meeting" in 100–150 words.*

a) A missing part of a story or an ending

- Grundlegende Voraussetzung für das Schreiben eines fehlenden Abschnitts, eines Texts oder eines Endes ist das sichere Textverständnis.
- Der zu verfassende Teil muss sich sowohl logisch aus der Textvorlage ergeben als auch kreative Elemente enthalten.
- Er darf nicht im Widerspruch zu Aussagen im Text oder zu Charaktereigenschaften stehen, die sich aus dem Text ableiten lassen.
- Daher ist es absolut notwendig, sowohl die beschriebene Situation als auch die Figuren zu verstehen und sich mit ihnen zu identifizieren. Nur so ist eine überzeugende Ergänzung der Textvorlage möglich.
- Oft erweist es sich als überzeugend, inhaltliche Elemente der Textvorlage aufzugreifen und zu verarbeiten.
- Neben inhaltlichen Aspekten ist die Sprache sehr wichtig, die sich möglichst wenig von der des Originaltextes unterscheiden sollte.

2. *The story "The Meeting" (pp. 94–96) has an open ending. Continue the story in about 150 words.*

b) Writing a dialogue

- Beachte die richtige Wiedergabe der direkten Rede, d. h. Anführungszeichen immer oben (auch am Anfang).
- Im Englischen steht ein Komma (statt Doppelpunkt) zwischen dem Satz, der die Rede einleitet, und der wörtlichen Rede.
- Gesprochenes ist oft weniger formell als Geschriebenes. Je nach Sprecher und Anlass ist also auch Umgangssprache möglich.
- Du musst einen geeigneten Anfang und ein passendes Ende des Gesprächs finden.
- Auch hier ist es äußerst wichtig, sich mit den Personen zu identifizieren (Alter, Charakter, Herkunft, daraus resultierende Sprache, Haltung).
- Manchmal ist es ratsam, eine Einführung zur Erläuterung der Situation zu schreiben, die aber kurz gehalten werden sollte.

TIPP

Markiere vor dem Schreiben des Dialogs wichtige Textstellen, die Informationen über die Charaktere und das Geschehen geben.

3. *Write a dialogue between Candy and her father after leaving Becky behind in about 300 words ("The Meeting", pp. 42–44).*

c) Writing a comment

- Unter *comment* versteht man eine schriftliche begründete Stellungnahme zu einem Thema, einer Aussage, einer Frage oder einem Cartoon.
- Sie besteht aus drei grundsätzlichen Teilen: *introduction* (Einleitung), *main part* (Hauptteil), *conclusion* (Schlussfolgerung).
- In der Einleitung wird die zur Diskussion stehende Aussage mit eigenen Worten wiedergegeben. Außerdem gibt sie eine Meinung dazu ab (Zustimmung oder Ablehnung).
- Im Hauptteil werden die Argumente und Gründe für die eigene Meinung mit Beispielen belegt und veranschaulicht.
- Der Schluss fasst die gesamte Argumentation noch einmal in einem wertenden Urteil zusammen.

1. *Comment on the following statement: "All people are equal, no matter who they are or where they come from." (300–450 words)*

d) Writing a review

- Rezensionen bzw. Kritiken kann man z. B. zu Filmen, Büchern oder Theaterstücken schreiben.
- Sie sollen wichtige Informationen wie Titel und Regisseur bei Filmen bzw. Autor, Titel und Verlag bei Büchern sowie das Erscheinungsjahr enthalten. (Hinweis: Diese Informationen findet man häufig im Internet.)
- Die Rezension enthält eine **kurze** Inhaltsangabe – jedoch ohne das Ende zu verraten (wenn nicht anders gefordert).
- Außerdem werden meist Angaben zu Genre (z. B. Krimi, Thriller, Liebesgeschichte) und Thema des Werks sowie zu den Hauptfiguren und deren Beziehungen zueinander gemacht.
- Bei einer Filmkritik bietet sich, wenn möglich, auch der Bezug auf das Buch an.
- Ganz wichtiger Bestandteil der Kritik ist die begründete Meinungsäußerung, d. h. Aussagen dazu, warum dir das Werk gefällt oder nicht, was daran besonders beeindruckt oder ob und warum du es weiterempfehlen würdest.
- Als gelungen kann eine Kritik gelten, wenn sie neugierig auf das Werk macht.

EXAMPLE

LIFE IS A WHEEL OF FORTUNE

In his movie "Match Point" (Hollywood 2005), Woody Allen pursues the idea of sheer luck as the key to success in our unpredictable lives and draws a cynical final conclusion.

Filmplakat „Match Point" (2005, Copyright: Cinetext)

Chris Wilton (Jonathan Rhys Meyers) wants to overcome his origins of Irish lower class. But having buried his hope of a career as a professional tennis player, he ends up teaching London's high class. Fortunately, Chris is a gentleman of very refined tastes who quickly becomes friends with the yuppie Tom Hewett (Matthew Goode).

Soon, Tom's pretty and sweet sister Chloe (Emily Mortimer) falls in love with the lover of Dostojevskian books, Italian operas and contemporary modern art. When she becomes Chris' girlfriend, she encourages him to pursue his career in her father's business. The culmination is their marriage. However, the romantic comedy turns into a satirical tragedy of crime without punishment. Scarlett Johansson, famous since Lost in Translation, convincingly performs the "femme fatale" Nola Rice who first blinds Tom, then Chris. The plot is developed according to the course of a tennis match unfolding the story in the opening scene. At the end, the match point decides the game and the film characters' fate in the film in an unexpected way. Woody Allen surprises his fans with an unusual setting (London instead of New York) and an epic narrative with gripping action. (231 words)

Vocabulary:
wheel of fortune – Glücksrad
refined – gebildet, kultiviert
Dostojevsky – russischer Schriftsteller, dessen Roman *„Schuld und Sühne" (Crime and Punishment)* zur Weltliteratur gehört
culmination – Höhepunkt, krönender Abschluss
unfold – darlegen
setting – Schauplatz
gripping – packend, fesselnd

1. *Write a review of a book or film you like.*

COMMENT ON A PICTURE

Adolph von Menzel (1815–1905), French Window (1845)

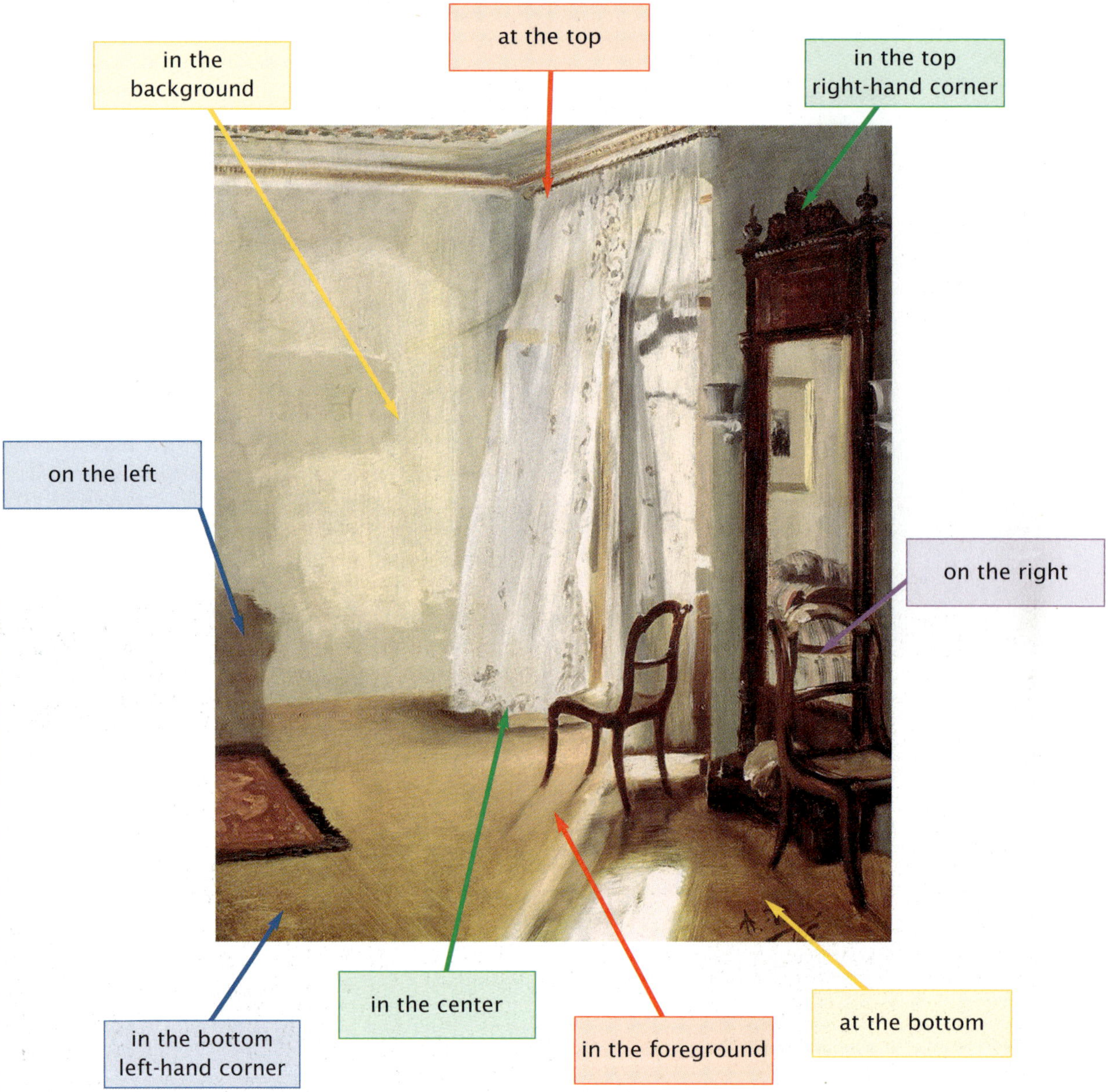

Bildbeschreibung

- Schau dir das Bild genau an und bestimme, was für eine Art Bild es ist, z. B. Gemälde *(painting)*, Zeichnung *(drawing)*, Foto *(photo)* oder Cartoon *(cartoon)*.
- Welche Situation wird im Bild dargestellt? Nutze für die Beschreibung des Bildes Wendungen, wie sie oben angeboten werden.
- Versuche Antworten auf die Fragen *wer, was, wo* und, wenn möglich, *wann* und *warum* zu geben.

- Um die Atmosphäre des Bildes zu beschreiben, untersuche folgende Merkmale: verwendete Farben, Gesichtsausdruck und Körpersprache, die Beziehung der abgebildeten Menschen oder Dinge zueinander bzw. ihre Anordnung.
- Was sagt dir der Titel des Bildes?
- Erschließe die Bedeutung von möglichen Symbolen.
- Überlege, ob vielleicht etwas im Bild fehlt und wenn ja, warum.
- Welche Wirkung hat die vom Künstler gewählte Perspektive auf dich?
- Wie wirkt das Bild auf dich? Gefällt es dir? Warum bzw. warum nicht?

1. *On page 48 you can see the picture "French window" by Adolph von Menzel.*

a) Describe the picture and interpret the situation. (200–300 words)

b) Do you like this picture? Why or why not? (100–150 words)

c) Imagine you see this painting when you are at an exhibition together with a friend. Write the conversation you might have. (250–400 words)

2. *Now have a closer look at the picture "Nighthawks" by the American artist Edward Hopper.*

a) Describe the picture and interpret the situation. (200–300 words)

b) Give reasons why you would or wouldn't like to be one of the people in the picture. (100–200 words)

Edward Hopper (1882–1967), Nighthawks (1943)

1) Einleitung

As we know ...	Wie wir wissen, ...
Research has shown that ...	Die Forschung hat gezeigt, ...
It is often claimed / said / stated that ...	Es wird oft behauptet / gesagt, ...
It is commonly / generally believed that ...	Allgemein glaubt man, ...
Today we are often confronted with the issue / problem of ...	Heutzutage sind wir oft mit dem Thema / Problem der / des ... konfrontiert
It goes without saying ...	Es versteht sich von selbst, ...

Meinungsäußerung

I would say ...	Ich würde sagen, ...
I am convinced that ...	Ich bin überzeugt (davon), dass ...
I personally believe / think that ...	Ich persönlich denke / glaube, dass ...
In my opinion / from my point of view ...	Meiner Meinung nach ...
It seems to me that ...	Es scheint mir, dass ...
My point of view is that ...	Meine Meinung ist, dass ...
Therefore I would say / do not think / cannot agree ...	Deshalb würde ich sagen / nicht denken / kann ich nicht zustimmen, ...

2) Hauptteil – Argumentation

Aufzählung

Firstly ... secondly ... thirdly	Erstens ... zweitens ... drittens
On the one hand ... on the other hand	Einerseits ... andererseits
First of all ... then ... finally ...	Zuallererst ... dann ... schließlich / zum Schluss ...
To begin / start with ...	Zuerst
The first (second, next, last) point I'd like to mention / make is ...	Den ersten (zweiten, nächsten, letzten) Punkt, den ich nennen möchte, ...
First and foremost ...	Zuallererst ...
Last but not least ...	Nicht zuletzt / nicht zu vergessen ...

Beispiele

For example / instance ...	Zum Beispiel ...
Let me give you a couple of examples ...	Lasst mich ein paar Beispiele nennen / anführen ...
Take for example ...	Nimm zum Beispiel ...
To illustrate this, ...	Um dies zu illustrieren, ...
... illustrates this point perfectly.	... veranschaulicht diesen Punkt perfekt.
You only have to think of / Just think of ...	Du brauchst nur mal an ... zu denken / Denk mal an ...

Ergänzungen

Furthermore / besides / in addition to this ...	Außerdem ...
Moreover ...	Überdies, ferner ...
Another / a further point ...	Ein weiterer Punkt ...
Apart from ...	Abgesehen von ...
It must also be said that ...	Man muss auch sagen, dass ...
In general / on the whole / generally speaking ...	Im Allgemeinen ...
As a rule ...	Normalerweise ...
When we have a closer look (at) ...	Wenn wir ... genauer betrachten, ...
I want to highlight / stress / emphasise ...	Ich möchte betonen / hervorheben, ...
It is important / vital to realise that ...	Es ist wichtig / unerlässlich zu erkennen, dass ...
Indeed ...	In der Tat / wirklich ...
It is certainly true that ...	Es ist sicherlich richtig, dass ...
It is (very) clear / certain that ...	Es ist (sehr) offensichtlich / klar / sicher, dass ...
... as everyone knows.	... wie jederman weiß.
This supports my argument that ...	Dies unterstützt mein Argument, dass ...
It is difficult to believe that ...	Es fällt einem schwer zu glauben, dass ...
... seems possible / likely / unlikely.	... scheint möglich / wahrscheinlich / unwahrscheinlich ...
In other words/To put it in another way ...	Mit anderen Worten / Anders gesagt ...

Gegenargumente und Einschränkungen

However ...	Jedoch ...
Although ...	Obwohl ...
There is no denying that ...	Es lässt sich nicht bestreiten, dass ...
On the contrary / In contrast / By comparison with ...	Im Gegenteil / Im Gegensatz / Verglichen mit ...
Whereas ...	Wohingegen / während ...
Despite / In spite of ...	Trotz ...
Nevertheless ...	Trotzdem / dennoch ...

3) Zusammenfassung

In short / Thus ...	Kurz gesagt / Folglich ...
To put it in a nutshell ...	Auf den Punkt gebracht ...
To summarise / sum up / conclude ...	Zusammenfassend / abschließend ...
All in all / In conclusion ...	Insgesamt / Zum Abschluss/ Abschließend ...
Therefore ...	Deshalb / daher ...
Having considered all these issues ...	Nachdem ich all diese Punkte betrachtet habe, ...
All these facts lead me to the conclusion that ...	All diese Punkte führen mich zu der Schlussfolgerung, dass ...

Gemma by Melvin Burgess

My parents are incompetent. They haven't got a clue. They think being a parent is like being an engineer or something – you do this, you do that, and this is the result you get at the other end. Someone ought to give parents lessons before they allow them to breed.

That night in the garage, we never did anything. I mean, I wanted to sleep with him. It would have been a nice way to say goodbye, and poor Tar could've done with a nice goodbye, really. That's to say, if I'd done it before, it would have been a nice way to say goodbye, but I don't know if the first time is the right way to say goodbye. But I might have done it anyway – for me, for him. It wasn't for either of us I didn't.

I only didn't do it for my parents. I wanted to be able to say, Look ... this was my boyfriend. He was in some really nasty trouble, he was really upset, he was hurt, he'd been beaten up by his dad for the nth time, he was running away and I spent the night with him because he needed some company.

And I think he might be in love with me.

But there was no sex, we never did that. It was just ... being close.

Is that human or what?

The only thing I regret is that I put my dad before Tar. I won't make that mistake twice.

When I got home the next day, all hell broke loose.

My dad was wagging up and down the room. 'There must be limits ... there must be rules!'

Mum was sitting on the edge of the chair with no lips trying not to cry.

'We all have to follow the rules, Gemma. When I forbid something I expect you to obey me ...'

I tried to smile at my mum but she looked the other way.

Then he came out with this real beauty. Listen to this: 'Her reputation is a girl's greatest asset ...'

Stone Age!

'What about her GCEs?' I said. 'What about her ability to put her lipstick on properly?'

My mum tried to bring the conversation into the real world.

'Darling, you're too young –' she began.

'She'll have to learn!'

'What are we going to do, Gemma? Your father's right, there have to be rules. Surely you can see that?'

'Where's David?' My father said. That's Tar. I christened him Tar, because he was always telling me off for smoking.

'You'll get tar in your lungs,' he kept saying.

'Ring up his house and find out,' I told my dad.

'I have. He's not come home. But his father's promised to give him what for when he does.'

I nearly said, He'll have a long wait, then. But I bit my tongue. 'He already has,' I told him. 'He beat him up again the night before last.'

Dad snorted. 'He got into another fight, you mean.'

Tar's dad's a teacher at one of the local high schools. You can see the way my dad's brain works. Teacher = good. Bad relationship with Tar = Tar's fault.

'He hits the bottle,' I told him. 'Go round and see him next time. You'll smell it. That's the sort of influence we young people have to look up to,' I said.

'Don't try and be clever with me!'

'Look ... Tar was upset. He just needed someone to stay with him. But there was no sex. Honest. All right?'

There was a pause in which my dad looked at me. You could see how furious he was. As if me being responsible was some sort of threat to his authority.

Then he said, 'Liar.'

(Melvin Burgess, Junk, Andersen Press, London, 1996)

Vocabulary:

incompetent – nicht zuständig, unfähig
have no clue – keine Ahnung haben
breed – brüten, *hier:* Kinder aufziehen
(all) hell breaks loose – (auf einmal) war der Teufel los, ging das Donnerwetter nieder *(bildlich)*
reputation – Ruf, Ansehen
GCEs – *(Prüfungen in englischen Schulen am Ende der 10. Klasse)*
christen – taufen
snort – schnauben
hit the bottle – „an der Flasche hängen", regelmäßig viel Alkohol trinken
threat – Bedrohung
liar – Lügner

1. *Read the text.*

2. *Choose one task for creative writing:*

a) *Write Gemma's diary entry for this day in which she reflects upon the night she spent with Tar as well as the scene with her parents when she came home. (about 200 words)*

b) *Tar has given Gemma an address she can write to so that they can keep in contact. Write Gemma's letter to Tar in which she tells him about returning home after their last night together. (about 200 words)*

c) *How does the story continue? (about 250 words)*

3. *"There must be limits ... there must be rules!" Must there be limits and rules for children, no matter if they are 5 or 15 years old? Write a comment (about 400 words).*

Grundvoraussetzungen

Neben dem Schreiben und dem Hörverstehen ist das Sprechen die wichtigste fremdsprachliche Fertigkeit. Sie hängt zwar mit dem Hören zusammen, sollte aber gezielt geübt werden. Zum Beispiel musst du Vokabeln beim Sprechen sehr schnell parat haben, also aktiv wissen. Für das Leseverständnis und teilweise auch für das Hören reichen dagegen Vokabeln, die du verstehen kannst, die aber nicht zu deinem produktiven Wortschatz gehören.
Das Sprechen ist eine sehr komplexe Tätigkeit. Es gehören mitunter viele Dinge dazu, dass dein Gesprächspartner dich versteht, nicht nur Sprachliches im engsten Sinne. Ihr müsst einen ähnlichen Kontext haben, der Sprecher muss z.B. wissen, was er als bekannt voraussetzen kann. Wenn die Redesituation von beiden gleichermaßen interpretiert wird, sind oft nicht viele Worte nötig („Ist der Platz neben Ihnen noch frei?", „Stört es Sie, wenn ich ein Fenster aufmache?" etc.). Mimik und Gestik sind in solchen Standardsituationen besonders wichtig.

TIPP

- *Zum angemessenen Sprechen gehören die Aussprache, die Betonung, die Intonation (= Veränderung des Tones nach Höhe und Stärke) sowie der Rhythmus. Sie lassen sich am besten durch konsequentes Üben des Hörverstehens, durch Nachsprechen und Mitsingen entwickeln. Höre bei deinen Lieblingssongs einmal genauer hin und finde heraus, worum es sich handelt. Summe nicht nur mit, sondern singe mit.*
- *Höre englischsprachige Radiosender und schau dir englischsprachige Fernsehprogramme an.*
- *Sieh dir englische Filme auf DVD an, benutze dabei möglichst nicht die deutschen Untertitel!*

- *Beim Sprechen ist deine Mitteilung wichtig. Sie sollte natürlich sachlich, lexikalisch und möglichst grammatikalisch korrekt sein.*
- *Der Adressat der Mitteilung ist ebenfalls bedeutsam. Von ihm hängt ab, welche Stilebene (förmlich, informell) du wählst.*
- *Wechsle nicht zwischen den stilistischen Ebenen und den Varianten des Englischen.*
- *Wenn du mehrere Sätze am Stück reden musst (Vortrag, Bericht, umfangreichere Stellungnahme im Unterricht etc.), überlege dir vorher, was du sagen möchtest und ordne deine Gedanken. Fertige Stichpunkte an.*

- *Suche dir einen Partner, mit dem du üben kannst.*
- *Zeichne euer Gespräch auf, um dich selbst zu hören und eventuell zu korrigieren.*
- *Übe am besten laut vor einem Spiegel, um auch deine Körpersprache zu kontrollieren.*

Wenn du aktiv an einem Gespräch, einer Diskussion, später auch an einer Debatte teilnehmen willst, brauchst du bestimmte sprachliche Mittel. Du kannst dich auf viele unterschiedliche Gesprächsanlässe vorbereiten, wenn du diese sprachlichen Mittel verinnerlichst. Ständiges Wiederholen und Anwenden am besten in Partnerarbeit oder Kleingruppe, zu Hause oder in der Schule, werden dich sehr unterstützen.

Notwendiges Vokabular

Expressing an opinion
- In my view/opinion
- My view/opinion is
- I feel/believe that
- I think
- I'm convinced

Giving reasons
- I think so because
- Well, it's a fact that
- The reason/point is
- This is why

Agreeing
- Yes, that's very true
- That's quite right
- I agree
- That's what I feel, too
- I think so, too

- *(informal)* Right! Sure! Great!
- Yes, definitely! Absolutely!

Half-agreeing
- Don't you think that
- Yes, I'd go along with that
- It seems to me that

Half-agreeing (continued)
- I'm not sure about that
- Mm, possibly, but
- Yes, I suppose so, but
- Well, yes, but
- Yes, perhaps you're right here/there
- Yes, you may have a point
- Yes, but on the other hand

Disagreeing
- I don't think so
- I'm afraid I can't agree with you
- No that's just not true
- No, that's absolutely wrong
- I disagree with that/you
- I can't go along with that
- That's out of the question

- *(informal)* Ridiculous! No way!

Asking for clarification
- Could you say that again, please?
- I beg your pardon?
- Pardon me?
- Sorry, I don't quite follow you
- What was that again?
- Do you mind repeating?
- Could you please explain what you mean?

TIPP

Typisch für den mündlichen Sprachgebrauch im Englischen sind die Kurzformen, z. B. I'm, that's, you're *etc.*

ÜBUNGSTIPP

Alle Übungen dieses Kapitels kannst du alleine, schriftlich oder mündlich bearbeiten. Besonders gut wäre es aber, wenn du jemanden findest, der dir die Texte und Fragen vorliest, damit du auch deine Hörfähigkeiten verbessern kannst. Am besten, du suchst dir einen Partner aus deinem Englischkurs, mit dem du die Übungen immer abwechselnd machst. Ihr könnt dann auch gegenseitig euren Lernerfolg kontrollieren.

1. *Rewrite the following expressions using the past tense.*

EXAMPLE *I'm convinced – I was convinced.*

a) My view is Britain is unique in its transport system.

b) I agree to let you go.

c) The point is most women and men want the right to work.

d) Don't you think that co-educational schools are better?

e) That's quite right.

f) Yes, I suppose so, but hosting the World Cup gives a great boost to tourism.

2. *Rewrite the following expressions as negative statements.*

EXAMPLE *I think so, too. I don't think so.*

a) That's what I feel, too.

b) I believe that chewing gum makes you clever.

c) I'm convinced the World Cup will make the country more attractive to visitors.

d) Yes, perhaps you're right there.

e) I agree with you that employers must introduce new working practices.

Talking about TRAVEL

A: What is your favourite country apart from your own?

B: I suppose I've a soft spot for Sweden.

A: Isn't it rather cold there?

B: Well yes, but if you visit it in June, it's extremely beautiful.

A: What do you like about it?

B: Above all, the feeling of space, the wonderful lakes and the thoughtful city planning. You have the impression that people are well looked after, whether they're young or elderly. They have good sports facilities, hospitals and schools. Prices are rather high, but maybe that's a good thing.

A: What do you mean?

B: I mean that the country isn't inundated with tourists. It hasn't been ruined by timeshare developments or scores of ugly hotels, bars and discos. It's just itself.

A: Is there anything to do or see?

B: Yes, plenty. Stockholm's among the most attractive capitals in Europe. You can visit an open-air museum and observe several different traditional crafts such as spinning wool, candle-making and glass-blowing. It's perfect for short outings – boat trips around the islands and visits to show-piece villages such as Sigtuna.

A: Where is that?

B: It's just a bus ride away from Stockholm. The high street in Sigtuna is simply charming. It's full of small shops which seem to be from another era. There's a delightful church and the view over the lake is magnificent.

A: And I gather it isn't a tourist village?

B: Well, yes and no. Sigtuna certainly attracts visitors, though you'll probably meet as many Swedes there as foreigners.

A: Where can I go after Stockholm?

B: There are many choices. You can travel north to see the midnight sun and to visit the polar bears. You can take the night train south west to Copenhagen, the home of Carlsberg beer, or else head south towards Berlin. You can take the ferry east to Finland, or take the seven hour train journey across the country to Gothenberg passing many spectacular lakes on the way.

Vocabulary:
have a soft spot for s.o./sth. – etwas mögen
city planning – Stadtplanung
sports facilities – Angebote zum Sporttreiben (Turnhallen, Sportplätze etc.)
inundate – überschwemmen, überfluten
timeshare development – Ferienhaussiedlung mit vielen verschiedenen Besitzern
candle – Kerze
outing – Ausflug

1. *Read the dialogue.*

2. *Go through the dialogue and pick out expressions you can use in other situations, too (at least ten).*

EXAMPLE *What is your favourite ...?*

3. *Imagine the situation where B would answer: "My dream country is Australia."*

EXAMPLE
A: What is your favourite country apart from your own?
B: I suppose I like Australia very much. I'm very interested in the smallest continent. It would be my dream to visit the outback and some of the great cities, especially Sydney.
A: Isn't it a rather rough country and very expensive for a student?
B: ...
A: What do you like most about it?
B: ...
A: Would you travel alone or in a group?
B: ...
A: Which kind of transport would you use to explore the country?

TIPP

Im Kapitel Lesen findest du viele Fakten über Sydney, die du als Argumente verwenden könntest (S. 66–68).

4. *Imagine a situation where you have to tell your friend about your favourite country.*

Vokabeln zur Strukturierung deiner Argumentation
Wenn du mehrere Argumente oder Aspekte aufzählen möchtest, helfen dir unter anderem folgende Wendungen.

Beginn
Firstly, ...
First of all, ...
The first thing to say is ...
Well, firstly ...
To begin with ...
I'd start by (+ ing-Form)
Let me begin by saying ...

Fortsetzung
There're two points/ problems here ...
Moreover ...
In addition ...
Furthermore ...
The next point is ...

Logischer Abschluss
As a result ...
The solution is ...
The best way to ...
There are many choices. You can ...
Alternatively ...
You see the alternative is ...
Consequently, ...
Therefore, ...
In conclusion, ...

Zeitlicher Abschluss
Finally ...
To close ...
Last but not least ...

Talking about FASHION

1. *Read the dialogue and underline all parts that express an opinion, disagreement or doubt or that ask for an opinion.*

A: In my opinion fashion is a complete waste of time, money and resources.

B: I disagree entirely. The world would be a very boring place without change.

A: Fashion doesn't only involve change. It's a very dishonest form of marketing based on artificial images which never translate into reality.

B: But everyone understands that the images are there to capture attention. People find them fun. Haven't you ever looked through a fashion magazine?

A: Only at the dentist's.

B: What about the glossy magazines which you get when you buy a Sunday newspaper? They're full of fashionable advertisements.

A: That's true, but don't you think they're a terrible waste of paper? How many people throw them straight into the dustbin?

B: A lot of people must read them and they don't add to the cost of the newspaper.

A: There are two points here. Firstly, the cost to the environment. Think of all the rain forests. Secondly, the advertiser may pay but the costs are passed on to the consumer.

B: That isn't strictly true. If a company can sell in bulk, prices can be brought down. You can't expect to sell unless the consumer knows that the product exists.

A: I wouldn't mind publicity if it told you something about the product, but by getting fashion models to market clothes and even cars you are hiding the truth. When I buy clothing I want to know if it's comfortable and how long it's going to last.

B: That may be your reason, but some people buy clothes because they want to look nice. Perhaps they have a special date or engagement. People have always liked dressing up.

A: That may be so, but traditional costumes were made to be worn more than once. What worries me is today's throw-away society where some people waste the world's precious resources while other people go without.

B: Well I don't see why you should blame the fashion industry for social injustice.

Vocabulary:
artificial – künstlich
glossy – glänzend
dustbin – Mülleimer
environment – Umwelt
sell in bulk – in großen Mengen verkaufen

2. *Now join the discussion and give your own views on the topic.*

ÜBUNGSTIPP

Du beherrschst (spätestens) jetzt Vokabular und Argumentationsstrukturen, um Themen wie „Reisen“ oder „Mode“ zu erörtern. Wenn du noch sicherer werden willst, musst du dir nun einen Partner suchen, mit dem du ähnliche Stoffe diskutieren kannst. Geeignete Themen und diskussionswürdige Probleme findest du im gesamten Band.

Until the year 2020 all private car traffic should be abolished.

Vocabulary:
abolish – abschaffen
damage – schaden
fine – Geldbuße
pollution – Verschmutzung
public transport – öffentlicher Nahverkehr
exhaust fumes – Abgase
car sharing – System, mit dem sich viele Menschen den Besitz eines oder mehrerer Autos teilen
rush hour – Tageszeit mit besonders hohem Verkehrsaufkommen
pedestrian zones – Fußgängerzone

1. *a) Find arguments for the proposal "Private car traffic should be abolished".*
b) Find arguments against the proposal "Private car traffic should be abolished".

2. *Choose one of the topics and find arguments agreeing with the statement.*

a) Smoking should be banned from school.
b) The impact of television is dangerous.

3. *Choose one of the topics and find arguments against the statements.*

a) Mixed classes should be abolished.
b) Violence and sex should not be shown on TV.

TIPP

Bei einem Thema, das du etwas ausführlicher diskutieren willst, solltest du dir die wichtigsten Argumente in Stichpunkten notieren – als Gedächtnisstütze und damit du eine vernünftige Reihenfolge in deine Argumentation bringst. Du kannst diesen Zettel auch dazu nutzen, zentrale Vokabeln, die du vorher nachschlagen musst, zu notieren.

In jedem Gespräch spielen Fragen eine wichtige Rolle. Fragen haben unterschiedliche Funktionen:

- Nachfrage (inhaltliche Klärung)
- Lenkung des Gesprächs
- Rhetorische Frage, auf die der Fragende nicht unbedingt eine Antwort erwartet, sondern in denen er meist eine eigene Position vertritt oder andeutet („glaubst du das wirklich?")

Wer viel fragt, übernimmt die Initiative im Gespräch und kann dessen Richtung bestimmen!

1. *Underline the questions in the dialogue "Fashion" (p. 52) and explain their function.*

2. *Give a short response to each of the following ten questions. Use words expressing agreement, half-agreement or disagreement.*

Fragentypen: Yes/No questions

a) Do you believe in horoscopes?
b) Do you think the Government should act to curb the power of media barons?
c) Would you consider sending your child to a grammar school?
d) Do you believe in a God who rewards good and punishes wrongdoing?
e) Do you think we should be tougher on crime?

Or Questions

a) Would you prefer your child to be educated privately or by the state?
b) Are you for or against the death sentence?
c) Would you rather go to a co-educational or single sex school?
d) What should or shouldn't be shown on TV?
e) Do you like your school or not?

3. *Give a short response to each of the following seven questions. Use the words and phrases that are used to express an opinion and give reasons.*

WH Questions (who, why, where, when, what)

a) What do you think are the causes of the increase of violence in our society?
b) What are the advantages and disadvantages of mixed classes?
c) Who are the media barons in your country?
d) Why don't some people believe in God?
e) When does the new programme start?

Negative Yes/No Questions

a) How about boarding schools? Don't they teach children how to live together?
b) What about the advantages and disadvantages of mixed classes? Don't you think it's better to learn together?

1. *Look at the telephone language below. Which phrases does a person use who is calling someone? Which does a person use who is being called?*

a) Hello, is that ...?
b) I'm afraid he / she is not in.
c) So sorry, I've got the wrong number.
d) Hello, this is from ...
e) I couldn't call earlier because your line was engaged.
f) I'll just find out if he / she is in.
g) Sorry, my phone was out of order.
h) Hold on a moment, please.
i) Is ... in?
j) ... speaking.
k) Could you give ... a message, please?
l) Can I speak to ... please?
m) I'll put you through to him / her.

person calling	***person being called***
a) ...	b) ...

2. *Take the part of B in the following phone call and fill in what he / she says. Be polite.*

A: Hello, could I speak to Mr. Miller, please?
B: *Herr Müller ist im Moment nicht da.*
A: Oh, I see. Have you got any idea when he'll be back?
B: *Du bist nicht sicher, wann er zurückkommt. Frage, ob du ihm etwas ausrichten darfst.*
A: Oh, if you would. Please. Could you ask him to call me back as soon as possible. It's about a DVD he ordered. It's quite urgent.
B: *Frage, ob Herr Müller die Nummer des Anrufers hat.*
A: Yes, I think so, too. But I'll give it to you again, just in case, it's 01736521412.
B: *Bestätige, dass du es richtig notiert hast.*
A: That's right.
B: *Frage nochmals nach dem Namen des Anrufers.*
A: My name is Susan Tailor.
B: *Bitte die Person, den Namen zu buchstabieren.*
A: That's T-a-i-l-o-r.
B: *Bedanke und verabschiede dich.*

3. *Find out suitable questions for the conversation on mobile phones.*

a) A: ______________________?
B: Yes, I have. I don't use it as much as I'd like, because I have to pay for it myself.

b) A: ______________________?
B: I use Cellnet and I've got to pay in advance – you know, with prepaid vouchers.

c) A: ______________________?
B: I have to admit they do at times. I could go mad when they ring in the cinema or in a restaurant. One rang the other day during a film I was at – that was very annoying.

Jetzt wird dir gezeigt, wie du effektiv präsentieren kannst (einen Vortrag oder ein Referat halten). Wenn du die Hinweise beachtest und anwendest, wird es dir gelingen, überzeugend zu präsentieren.

Allgemeine Hinweise:

a) Wie beim Schreiben soll eine mündliche Präsentation (ein Vortrag oder Referat) eine gedankliche Gliederung aufweisen, bestehend aus:
- Introduction / Einleitung, in der du mitteilst, worum es geht
- Main Part / Hauptteil, in dem du die wichtigsten Aspekte des Themas behandelst
- Conclusion / Summary / Zusammenfassung, in der du wesentliche Punkte zusammenfasst und eventuell deine Meinung äußerst

TIPP

➡ *Überlege dir eine sinnvolle Reihenfolge für die Inhalte des Hauptteils, Zwischenüberschriften können dabei hilfreich sein.*

b) Informationsbeschaffung:
- Notiere, was du bereits über das Thema weißt!
- Deine eigene Meinung und Erfahrung allein reichen nicht aus, du musst dir unbedingt Informationen beschaffen!
- Nutze eine Bibliothek oder das Internet.
- Lies englische Quellen, dein Vortrag wird auch auf Englisch gehalten!
- Erinnere dich an die Lesetechnik *Skimming* (überfliegendes Lesen). Du wirst nicht alle gefundenen Informationen gründlich lesen können.

c) Anfertigen von Notizen:
- Beschränke dich auf die wichtigsten Informationen!
- Entscheide, zu welchen Aspekten du vertiefende Informationen geben möchtest!
- Suche nach Schlüsselwörtern in deinem Recherche-Material, lies entsprechende Passagen genauer und notiere stichpunktartig! Tipp: Informiere dich im Kapitel „Lesen“ noch einmal über die Lesetechniken!
- Bei dem Anfertigen der Notizen nie die Quellenangabe vergessen, egal ob Buch oder Internetseite. Es ist meistens mühevoll oder unmöglich, diese nachträglich zu rekonstruieren.

d) Medieneinsatz:
Gezielter Medieneinsatz lässt jede Präsentation lebendiger erscheinen.
Besonders geeignete Medien können sein:
- Fotos (Poster), Zeichnungen, Statistiken, Diagramme, Landkarten, die du auch mit dem OHP verwenden kannst
- Falls du einen Beamer zur Verfügung hast: Powerpoint-Präsentation, digitale Fotos, Filme oder Tondokumente
- Entwurf eines Tafelbildes
- CDs, Kassetten, Videos

e) Handout:
Ein Handout für deine Mitschüler erleichtert diesen die Orientierung.
Auf dem Handout müssen mindestens das Vortragsthema, die Gliederung des Vortrags und seine wichtigsten Aspekte erscheinen. Du kannst auch (kurze) Texte oder Bilder, die du besprechen willst, dort aufnehmen. Eine Vokabelliste mit schwierigen Wörtern sowie die Angaben der genutzten Quellen gehören ebenfalls dazu. Vergiss nicht, deinen Namen und das Datum des Vortrags auf das Handout zu setzen!

Phrases to introduce your topic

I want to point out ...
Our topic is ...
The centre of interest is ...
I want to outline the main idea of ... by ...
My presentation is about ...
First, I'd like to talk about ...

General Phrases:

In my view ...
To my mind ...
Now let's turn to ...
The next point I would like to make is ...
Another interesting thing about ... is ...
The comments range from ... to ...

Phrases at the end of the presentation

To sum up, we can ...
So, to go over the main points again, ...
So much for ...
Finally, I'd like to say a few words about ...
Does anyone have any questions?

TIPP

Dein Auftreten bei der Präsentation ist fast genauso wichtig wie der Inhalt:
- *Rede klar und laut.*
- *Versuche frei zu reden, Ablesen ist sehr ermüdend für die Zuhörer.*
- *Rede nicht zu schnell.*
- *Mach kurze Sprechpausen, vor allem hinter wichtigen Sätzen und bei gedanklichen Absätzen.*
- *Schau die Zuhörer zwischendurch an, starre nicht durch sie hindurch oder an die Decke.*
- *Rhetorische Fragen lockern auf und nehmen die Aufmerksamkeit der Zuhörer in Anspruch (direkte Anrede).*

Poster or Collage
Im Unterricht und in Prüfungssituationen wirst du dich zu Postern oder Collagen äußern müssen. Generell gelten die Dinge, die oben beschrieben wurden.
Hier nur noch kleine Ergänzungen.

Phrases to describe your collage / your poster
With our collage / poster we would like to concentrate on ...
Take a good look at the picture and you can see ...
The picture shows ...
In the centre of the picture there is / are ...
On the left / right there is / are ...
At the top / bottom of the picture there is are ...
In the top left-hand corner you can see ...
In the bottom right-hand corner you can see ...
In the foreground / background there is / are ...
In the middle there is ...
The whole photo shows ...

TIPP

Im Kapitel „Schreiben" findest du auch weitere Informationen zur Bildbeschreibung *(S. 48 f.)*

1. *Read these pairs of sentences. Cross out the sentences with phrases that you would not use in a presentation.*

a) My presentation is about how to prepare a speech properly.
b) Let me tell you about the most important things needed to prepare a speech properly.
c) OK, listen carefully now. This means having an easy-to-remember structure and good, clear notes that you can read under stress.
d) First, have an easy-to-remember structure and good, clear notes that you can read under stress.
e) Now let's turn to another point. Practise the speech several times out loud.
f) I hope that you all know you should practise the speech several times.
g) You must keep in mind that you should ask a good friend to listen and give you feedback.
h) Another interesting thing about preparing a presentation is that you should ask a good friend to listen and give feedback.
i) The next point I'd like to make is: Be sure you learn the opening sentence by heart.
j) You have to learn the opening sentence by heart.
k) Finally, I'd like to say get to the room early and check that everything is available if you want to use visual aids.
l) What I'm trying to say is if you want to use visual aids, get to the room early and check that everything is available.
m) Finally, I'd like to say a few words about internal encouragement ...
n) What you should know is internal encouragement can help you, too.
o) Does anyone have any questions?
p) Do you all agree with my points on how to prepare a speech properly?

TEST: SPRECHEN

Das kannst du jetzt:
Du bist in der Lage, dich zu bestimmten Themen strukturiert zu äußern.
Du weißt, wie du Informationen bekommst und verarbeitest.
Dir ist klar, wie man sich in Gesprächen, Diskussionen, Debatten und Vorträgen professionell verhält.

1. *The following expressions can be used in a discussion. In which of the columns would you put them?*

- I think so, too.
- Yes, but on the other hand
- In my opinion
- The point is
- That's out of the question
- What was that again?
- Yes, perhaps you're right here
- I beg your pardon?
- Well, yes, but
- I'm not sure about that.
- Sorry, I don't quite follow you.
- Ridiculous!
- I'm afraid I can't agree with you.
- Yes, I'd go along with that
- Don't you think that
- I can't go along with that
- That's very true.
- It's a fact that
- That's quite right
- I'm convinced
- It seems to me that

Expressing my opinion	Giving reasons	Agreeing	Disagreeing	Half-agreeing	Asking for clarification

TEST: SPRECHEN

2. *Work with a partner and have a lively discussion about the topic "Smoking is fun".*

The following arguments will help you:

Pros	Cons
smoking is fun, relaxes	smoking is dangerous
you feel grown-up	bad for your health
you are "in"	too expensive
you've got something in your hand	too young for smoking in public
it tastes good	law forbids you to smoke
friends smoke	smoker's cough
you feel free	fingers and teeth turn brown
can't stop anyway	many die of lung cancer caused by smoking
non-smokers get lung cancer, too	better fat than dead
non-smokers spend their money on other things	anti-social: smokers make healthy people feel ill
non-smokers get fat	clothes smell of smoke
parents/teachers smoke	your smoke causes cancer in others

EXAMPLE *At a party:*
A girl asks a boy for a cigarette and they start talking.

Girl: Hello, have you got a cigarette for me?
Boy: Oh, sorry. I don't have any cigarettes. I don't smoke any more.
Girl: Oh, but smoking is fun, isn't it? Firstly it is relaxing, secondly it looks cool.
And I feel free.
Boy: Don't you think there are other opportunities to relax or to be cool?
Girl: ...

Parts of speech – Wortarten

Prefixes – Häufig verwendete Vorsilben im Englischen und ihre Bedeutung

prefix	*example*	*meaning*
anti-	anti-terror	opposed to, against
co-	cooperation	together with
counter-	counter argument	opposite, against
cyber-	cybercafé	connected with electronic communication networks
dis- il- im- in- ir- un-	disagree illegal impossible infinite irregular unknown	} not, the opposite of
ex-	ex-husband	former
inter-	international	between, from one to another
mega-	megabyte	very large or great
mis-	misunderstanding	bad or wrong (incorrect)
non-	non-alcoholic	not
re-	retell	again

Suffixes – Häufig verwendete Nachsilben zur Wortbildung im Englischen

nouns		*adjectives*	
suffix	*example*	*suffix*	*example*
-ance -ence	attendance confidence	-able	comfortable
-ancy -ency	expectancy emergency	-al	technical
-dom	wisdom, kingdom	-ative	creative
-er	teacher	-ese	Chinese
-ess	actress	-est	honest
-hood	neighbourhood	-ful	wonderful
-(i)an	musician	-ic	traumatic
-ics	mathematics	-ish	childish
-ion	presentation	-ive	explosive
-ism	capitalism	-less	harmless
-ist	psychologist	-(o)logical	technological
-ity	dignity	-ous	poisonous
-isation/-ization	globalisation	-some	awesome
-ment	improvement		
-ness	weakness		
-ology	technology		
-or	visitor		
-ship	relationship		

1. *Use prefixes to form new words.*

regular, literate, competent, unity, helmet, interpret, action, fortunately, hero, smoker, wife, fortune, star, dependent, president, net, relevant, mortal, ability, definite, comfortable, existence, honest, like, septic, personal, education, happy

2. *Complete the table using or omitting suitable suffixes.*

verb	noun	adjective
globalize		
		communicative
	talker / talk	
	usefulness / usage	
relate		
		organizational
		acting
weaken		
	trauma	
		computerized
inform		

3. *Complete the sentences by adding prefixes or suffixes from the above lists to the words given in the boxes. The context will help you.*

smoking, appeared, responsible, regular, happy, using

a) You must learn the past tense forms and past participles of the ______ verbs.
b) She likes taking risks, but sometimes she is really ______.
c) Being a chain smoker, I would never go to a ______ restaurant.
d) He was ______ when he got to know that his friend wouldn't come to his party.
e) Teenagers are often blamed for ______ drugs.
f) I can't find my keys, they have ______ again.

friend, develop, talk, alcohol, child, fashion

g) My dad hasn't always lived in London, he spent his ______ in the country.
h) A child's ______ can strongly be influenced by its surroundings/environment.
i) He had a few ______ with other boys in his neighbourhood.
j) I've never met such a ______ person, it seems as if he never stops talking.
k) She wears trousers which were ______ at least 30 years ago.
l) Drinking alcohol regularly can lead to ______.

Das *simple present*

Mit dem *simple present* (einfache Gegenwart) spricht man über regelmäßig stattfindende Dinge und Handlungen, über Tatsachen, Gewohnheiten oder dauerhafte Zustände.
Typische Signalwörter für diese Zeitform sind: *always, usually, often, sometimes, never, every day / month /..., regularly, on Tuesdays.*
Man bildet das *simple present* durch den einfachen Infinitiv des Verbs. In der dritten Person Singular wird *-s* oder *-es* an das Verb angehängt; Verben, die auf Konsonant + *-y* enden, verändern sich in der dritten Person Singular in *-ies:*

I take ➠ it takes *we go ➠ she goes* *they try ➠ he tries*

Um Fragen oder negative Aussagen zu bilden, verwendet man das Hilfsverb *do* mit dem Infinitiv.

Do you like school? / Does she always walk the dog?
I don't like school very much. / She doesn't walk the dog every day.

Das *present progressive*

Mit dem *present progressive* (Verlaufsform) spricht man über Handlungen, die zum Zeitpunkt des Sprechens passieren oder die über einen längeren Zeitraum in der Gegenwart (nicht unbedingt zum Zeitpunkt des Sprechens) stattfinden. Die Verwendung dieser Zeitform ist aber nur bei Verben möglich, die eine Tätigkeit *(go, sing, make)* oder einen Vorgang *(become, get)* ausdrücken.
Typische Signalwörter sind *(right) now, at the moment, just.*
Man bildet das *present progressive,* indem man eine Form von *be* verwendet und *-ing* an das Verb anhängt.

go ➠ she is going *take ➠ I am taking* *try ➠ we are trying*

ACHTUNG

Einige Verben erscheinen in der Regel nicht in der Verlaufsform: Verben der Wahrnehmung (feel, smell, sound, look, taste); *Verben des Gefühls* (love, hate, want, wish, like, refuse); *Verben, die geistige Prozesse ausdrücken* (think, believe, realize, mean, agree, know, forget, remember); *Verben, die Besitzverhältnisse ausdrücken* (own, belong, possess); *modale Hilfsverben* (can, must, may, shall, will) *sowie* be *(im Sinne von Existenz) und* have *(im Sinne von Besitz).*

1. *Put in the correct form of the verb – simple present or present progressive.*

"Original Sound"

The club _____ (fill) up fast on Friday nights. It is not different on this Friday. The crowd _____ (move) in rhythm to the pulsating beat as the DJ _____ (manipulate) his turntables and _____ (create) an irresistible groove propelled by a driving beat. As the lights flash, two women _____ (appear) on stage. While one woman _____ (sing) a haunting melody, the other _____ (call) out to the audience and then begins to rap about her life. The words _____ (speak) about drugs, gangs and violence, being lost and being found and surviving life off the reservation. The three people on stage _____ (form) a group called *Original* that _____ (gain) acclaim in the city for their compelling blend of hip-hop

and native rhythms. John Burnwood, the DJ and spokesperson for the group ______ (be) an eighteen-year-old Aboriginal living in Winnipeg, Canada. He is currently ______ (share) a small, dilapidated house in the north end of the city with his twin sisters Jessie and Wendy who are also members of *Original*. John's Cree heritage ______ (play) a vital role in his daily life and he ______ (attribute) the spiritual practices of his people with providing him the strength to cope with the urban poverty that typifies his neighbourhood. "It ______ (to be) easy to become lost here," states John, "I ______ (go) to school still, but I know a lot of guys who ______ (go) to jail. In this neighbourhood, if you are Indian, you have a higher chance of going to prison than graduating from High School."
John and his sisters started *Original* two years ago. "We ______ (find) our inspiration from the stories of our people, both past and present and because we all ______ (love) hip hop, it was a natural progression to mix it with the beats we heard at the Pow-wows. And rap is the perfect music for us because it combines rhythm and story-telling."
"It was from going to Pow-wows with my Dad that I found my talent for music and participating in the Sweat lodges gave me a sense of my importance and my future. A lot of kids ______ (not know) the stories of our people, they ______ (not have) respect for themselves and so they ______ (fall) into crime because it ______ (give) them a sense of importance." When asked about the audiences' reactions to their music, John hesitates before answering. "Sometimes I ______ (think) that just seeing the three of us on stage shocks people. People ______ (not can) always figure us out, but once I start mixing, people start dancing and when people dance, they open their minds. So when they ______ (hear) Jessie and Wendy ______ (sing), they are already open to an experience and that is what we try to give them."

Vocabulary:
turntable – flat round part of a record player
acclaim – public praise for s.o. or sth.
dilapidated – old and in a bad condition
Sweat lodge – indian sauna, *here:* dance hall, disco

2. *Simple present or present progressive? Fill in the gaps using the right tense.*

a) Joan and I ______ (sit) at the fireplace and ______ (look) into the fire. We ______ (wear) shorts and T-shirts. It ______ (be) still very warm although it ______ (be) almost midnight.
b) "What ______ (think) you about, Claire?" Joan ______ (ask) me.
c) "I ______ (think) about Steven. I ______ (miss) him and I ______ (wonder) what he ______ (do) right now," I ______ (say) and I ______ (be) happy that I ______ (get) a chance to talk about him.
d) My parents ______ (not like) Steven because they ______ (think) that he ______ (not have) a decent job.
e) He ______ (work) at a fast food restaurant at the moment.
f) Sometimes he ______ (ask) me for money, then I ______ (give) him some because I ______ (come) from a well-off family.

Im Englischen gibt es verschiedene Möglichkeiten, über Zukünftiges zu sprechen. Neben der Verwendung der *future tenses* können auch Zeitformen der Gegenwart mit Signalwörtern *(tomorrow, next year, later today, this evening, tonight, some day)* auf Handlungen in der Zukunft verweisen.

Das *will-future*

Das *will-future* benutzt man, um über Ereignisse in der Zukunft zu sprechen, die wahrscheinlich sind und vermutlich passieren werden. Außerdem drückt es spontane Entschlüsse aus. Es wird gebildet durch *will* + Infinitiv.

When I am 18, I will get my driver's licence.
I'll help you after supper.
Shall we dance? (Do you want to dance?) ➠ für spontane Vorschläge

Das *going-to-future*

Man benutzt das *going-to-future,* um feste Vorhaben in der Zukunft auszudrücken. Dabei ist eine Zeitangabe nicht unbedingt nötig. Man bildet die Zeitform, indem man eine Form von *be* + *going to* + Infinitiv verwendet.

She is going to talk to your maths teacher tomorrow.
I'm going to read that book (this summer).

Das *present progressive* als Ausdruck der Zukunft

Alternativ zum *going-to-future* kann das *present progressive* in Aussagen verwendet werden, die einen festen Plan ausdrücken. Dabei wird eine Zeitangabe der Zukunft gemacht:

He is moving to Canada this summer.
I am getting married tomorrow.

Das *simple present* als Ausdruck der Zukunft

Das *simple present* wird im Zusammenhang mit Zukünftigem verwendet, wenn es um Zeitpläne (TV / Kino /...), Programme und festgelegte Termine geht. Auch hierbei wird eine Zeitangabe gemacht:

The game is on television at 4:00 this afternoon.

Das *future progressive*

Diese Zeitform verwendet man, um über Ereignisse in der Zukunft zu sprechen, die sich einfach ergeben. Sie bezieht sich auch oft auf eine Zeitspanne in der Zukunft, während der eine Begebenheit oder Handlung stattfindet, aber nicht abgeschlossen wird. Sie wird gebildet durch *will be* + Verb + *-ing.*

In a year from now, she'll be going to school.
Please don't call us between 5:00 and 6:00, we will be watching the news.

Das *future perfect*

Diese Zeitform zeigt an, dass Ereignisse und Handlungen vor einem bestimmten Zeitpunkt in der Zukunft beendet sein werden. Sie wird gebildet durch *will have* + Partizip Perfekt (dritte Verbform).

I will have done it by Sunday.
Do you think the problem will have been solved by then?

1. *Fill in the correct verb forms in the right future tense.*

A year "Down Under"

Each year, hundreds of teens from across Germany participate in International exchange programs. Popular choices for students include Canada, the United States, the United Kingdom and Ireland. The international exchange program provides teens with a year long opportunity to live in an English-speaking environment and to experience first-hand English culture. Like many of her peers, Allison Schmidt is excited about participating in the program. However, unlike any of her fellow students, Allison's exchange experience (1) ______ (be) one long trip down under.

In just a few short weeks, Allison Schmidt (2) ______ (go) to Australia for an international Student Exchange program where she (3) ______ (live) in Wallogong, New South Wales, just outside of Sydney. "I've always wanted to go to Australia and now I (4) ______ (actually/live) there and ______ (go) to school too!" exclaims Allison. "I spoke with my host family and they have already told me that I (5) ______ (see) kangaroos and koalas every day. And they (6) ______ (have) a 'Barbie' on the beach for me when I get there. Of course, we (7) ______ (go) to Sydney, but what I really hope to do is to go scuba diving at the Great Barrier Reef in Queensland."

But it won't be all barbies and 'roos for Allison, "It (8) ______ (be) very exciting, but it' (9) ______ (be) hard too" declares Allison. "I (10) ______ (be) in an Australian School and I don't know if anyone (11) ______ (speak) German. My English is OK, but having to speak it all the time (12) ______ (be) really tough. My sister told me that after a few weeks, I (13) ______ (talk) like the Crocodile Hunter, but I don't know if I (14) ______ even (be able to) understand the teachers. If that happens, I don't know what I (15) ______ (do)."

Although participants are often excited to explore their host countries, the International Exchange program focuses mainly on educational achievements. Allison's year in Wallogong (16) ______ (feature) an accelerated Academic program that includes courses in Calculus, English Literature, History and Foreign languages. However, the heavy course load does not daunt Allison.

"This (17) ______ (be) the greatest experience I've ever had," states Allison. "Even though I (18) ______ (miss) my family and friends, I think it (19) ______ (be) fantastic. Maybe my sister is right," muses Allison. "In a year, I (20) ______ (speak) more English than I could have imagined possible. I (21) ______ (be surrounded) by Australians, I (22) ______ (experience) a totally different culture and I (23) ______ (learn) to speak English, just like they do down under!"

EXPRESSING THE FUTURE

2. *Answer the questions using the correct future tense.*

a) Where exactly is Allison going?
b) What kind of animals will she see?
c) Who will she miss when she is in Australia?
d) What is she excited about doing?
e) What does she think will be difficult about the experience?
f) What courses will she be taking?
g) How many students are going to Australia?

3. *Decide whether you should use the going-to future or the will-future. Then write down the complete dialogues.*

a) *Bob:* My brother and I / spend three weeks in the Canadian Rockies this summer.
Tim: What / you / do there?
Bob: We / do a course in bungee jumping.
Tim: Wow! That / be fun!

b) *Gavin:* Oh, I / certainly fail my English exam.
Emma: Don't worry so much. I'm good in English. I / help you.
An hour later:
Gavin (to his mother): Emma / help me study for my English exam.

c) *Mum:* You / work all night? It's almost 10! You / be very tired tomorrow if you don't stop now.
Liz: I / go to bed after this exercise.
Mum: OK, I / be back in ten minutes to see if you're in bed then.

Es gibt verschiedene Zeitformen im Englischen, um Vergangenheit auszudrücken.

Das *simple past*

Man benutzt das *simple past,* um über etwas zu berichten, das in der Vergangenheit stattgefunden hat und abgeschlossen ist. Außerdem werden Handlungsfolgen (z. B. in Erzählungen) im *simple past* wiedergegeben. Die typischen Signalwörter verweisen auf eine spezifische Zeit in der Vergangenheit, z. B. *yesterday, last week /..., a year /... ago, in 1988.*

Man bildet die Form, indem man bei regelmäßigen Verben *-ed* oder *-d* an den Infinitiv anhängt. Unregelmäßige Verben haben eigene *past tense* Formen, die man wie Vokabeln lernen muss.

phone ➡ *phoned*	*take* ➡ ***took***
love ➡ *loved*	*cut* ➡ ***cut***
cry ➡ *cried*	*go* ➡ ***went***

Das *simple present perfect*

Mit dem *simple present perfect* gibt man Handlungen wieder, die gerade beendet sind. Im britischen Englisch wird dabei häufig das Signalwort *just* verwendet (im amerikanischen Englisch benutzt man nach *just* oft auch das *simple past*).

Das *simple present perfect* beschreibt auch Handlungen oder Ereignisse, die schon beendet sind, aber Auswirkungen auf die Gegenwart haben. Außerdem wird es verwendet, wenn etwas schon einmal, häufig oder noch nie passiert ist.

Typische Signalwörter für eine Zeitspanne in der Vergangenheit sind *for* und *since.* Ohne eine bestimmte Zeitangabe sind typische Signalwörter *never, ever, always, already, still, so far, until now, (not) yet, recently.*

Man bildet die Zeit durch eine Form des Hilfsverbs *have* und das Partizip Perfekt.

*Mark **has** just phon**ed**. He **has** finish**ed** his homework and is ready to play now.*
***Have** you ever **seen** a whale? – Yes, I**'ve seen** lots.*

Das *present perfect progressive*

Diese Zeitform betont die Dauer einer Handlung und drückt aus, dass etwas in der Vergangenheit begonnen hat, aktuell andauert und vielleicht auch noch in der Zukunft weitergehen wird.

Typische Signalwörter sind hier ebenfalls oft *for* und *since.*

Die Zeitform wird gebildet durch eine Form von *have* + Partizip Perfekt + Verb + *-ing*

*Oh dear, what **have** you **been** do**ing** all morning?*
*She **has been** surf**ing** the Internet for ages.*

Das *past perfect*

Um innerhalb der Vergangenheit Vorzeitigkeit auszudrücken, benutzt man das *past perfect.* Es zeigt an, dass eine Handlung in der Vergangenheit vor einer anderen in der Vergangenheit liegenden abgeschlossenen Handlung *(simple past)* stattgefunden hat.

Die Zeitform wird gebildet durch *had* + Partizip Perfekt (dritte Verbform).

*He **had** already **done** his homework when I got home.*

TIPP

Übersicht über die Bildung der Zeitformen

Simple Present *infinitive* (3rd person *-s!*)	**Present Progressive** *is/are* + verb-*ing*	
Simple Past *-ed* (and irregular verbs!)	**Past Progressive** *was/were* + verb-*ing*	
Present Perfect *have/has + past participle*	**Present Perfect Progressive** *have/has been* + verb-*ing*	
Past Perfect *had + past participle*	**Past Perfect Progressive** *had been* + verb-*ing*	
Future Simple *will* + infinitive	**Future Progressive** *will + be* + verb-*ing*	**Future Perfect** *will + have + past participle*

1. *Simple past or present perfect? Put the verbs in brackets into the correct form. Be careful: sometimes the passive form is needed.*

MODEL UNITED NATIONS CONFERENCE

Two days ago six Year 10 students from Millingdale Middle school 1) ____ (take part in) the Model United Nations Conference, 2) ____ (hold) in New York City. "The experience 3) ____ (be) fantastic!" said James So, the star of the show, who 4) ____ only just ____ (admit) that before flying out of London Heathrow airport, he 5) ____ (feel) so nervous, he 6) ____ (consider) catching the next train home to the safety of his room. Fortunately for the Indian Delegation (represented by Millingdale), he 7) ____ (overcome) his anxiety.

James' debating skills 8) ____ (earn) him much praise so far. This 9) ____ (confirm) in New York where he 10) ____ (win) the Best Speaker Award at the Conference. Public speaking 11) ____ (teach) James to think quickly and logically on his feet. It 12) ____ (give) him an opportunity to learn about political, social and global issues which affect us all. Moreover, he 13) ____ (gain) greater self confidence.

Since James 14) ____ (begin) debating in year 8, first as a member of the debating society and then in year 9 for the MUN group, his overall grades 15) ____ (improve). "I 16) ____ (strengthen) my reading, writing, listening and speaking abilities. Until now, preparing for debates 17) ____ (be) similar to revising for exams but far more exciting: Yes, I would highly recommend debating to my fellow students. It's absolutely awesome! I can't believe that I 18) ____ (visit) the UN building and 19) ____ (have) a chance to meet with international UN representatives, both the professionals as well as their 'younger' counterparts," 20) ____ (report) James, beaming with pride.

2. *Read the text below. Then do task a).*

1) Information and communications technology (ICT) has revolutionized the world we live in. As a result, all individuals, including those less privileged and in developing countries, should enjoy access to the resources and digital opportunities that ICT allows.

2) Samal Ali, a 16 year old Malaysian, living in Kuala Lumpur, has been surfing the net and building web sites since he was 14. Despite his humble origins, Samal has found a way to broaden his interest in computer technology. His parents could not afford to buy him a computer so he decided to approach an insurance company near his school and offer his services. In exchange for doing odd jobs, he has gained access to one of the in-house computers. The initial half an hour per day has since increased to several hours and what started out as "playing around" has now developed into a lucrative part-time job for Samal.

a) *In paragraphs 1) and 2) underline all the verb forms in the present perfect in red and in the present perfect progressive in blue. Give reasons for the choice of tense.*

b) *Now go on reading paragraphs 3) and 4) and put the verbs in brackets in the simple present perfect or present perfect progressive. Sometimes you have to use the passive form.*

3) He ______ a) (carry out) data entry tasks, ______ b) (troubleshoot) when there are technical difficulties and ______ c) (build) web sites for the company as well as many of their clients for the past two years. Although, the company ______ d) (not always comply) with the Malaysian employment laws, there is often a ready loophole somewhere. Samal maintains he ______ e) (not be exploit) in any way. On the contrary, he feels he ______ f) (be reward) for his efforts. Once he ______ g) (complete) his work duties, he may do research for school projects and finish homework tasks using the computer.

4) At times, Mr and Mrs Ali worry that Samal ______ h) (neglect) his studies. Yet, the extra income ______ i) (prove) a welcome contribution for the family. For some time now Samal's parents ______ j) (flathunt). Their present living quarters, a 35 square meter flat, can barely accommodate the needs of a family of four. Samal ______ k) (scan) the on-line real estate advertisements for possibilities. Normally, a family of their social and economic status would not have access to these ads. With a little luck, the Ali family may succeed in improving their standard of living and benefiting from ICT.

Vocabulary:
troubleshoot – Probleme lösen
loophole – Schlupfloch
real estate – Immobilien (-Handel)

Interview with Shakira – Mixed Tenses

3. *Using the prompts below, write the interview between reporter Anne Peters and the Latin pop star idol, Shakira. Be careful to use the right tenses. Signal words will help. Feel free to add your own ideas to make the interview sound more authentic.*

(Foto: Reuters/Corbis)

TIPP

Hilfen zur Bildung der Zeitformen findest du auf S. 76 und zur Satzstellung unter dem Punkt Word order *auf S. 90.*

EXAMPLE *Reporter – Question: how long/sing*
Shakira – Answer: since childhood
Q: How long have you been singing?

Q: when/start/write/own songs
A: 8 years old

Q: (S.'s father is Lebanese) ever/visit/Lebanon
A: yes/Arabic sounds/influence my music

Q: true/Gabriel Garcia Marquez (Nobel Prize winning Colombian writer) /fan
A: yes/be a wonderful man/very encouraging

Q: hear/you/take/interest in/politics
A: since I be Colombian born/politics/always/be important/live in Colombia/be involved in politics

Q: you able/retain Latin American creativity/new English language songs on Laundry Service album
A: yes/write/English/challenge/spent long time/read poetry first

Q: can we/expect/hear/more English songs
A: definitely/not mean I not also continue/write songs in Spanish

Q: one final question before/time run out/when you launch next album.
A: much sooner than you think

Q: thank you for time/we look forward to new release
A: appropriate reply and polite goodbye

Simple past and past progressive

4. *Put the verbs in brackets in the correct form of the simple past or past progressive.*

a) While Sam ______ (play) the piano, his teacher suddenly ______ (sneeze).
b) I ______ (travel) to Munich the day Princess Diana ______ (die).
c) Many students ______ (study) for the Maths test when the fire alarm ______ (go off).
d) Just as the Prime Minister ______ (deliver) his speech, a bomb ______ (explode) at a nearby subway station.
e) When the Madonna concert ______ (begin), Jane and her friends ______ still ______ (sit) on the train to London.
f) David Beckham ______ (raise) his arms in victory when the referee ______ (declare) a foul.
g) When I ______ (be) young, my parents ______ always ______ (nag) me about my homework and now I do the same with my children.
h) Since traffic ______ (move) so slowly, Mr Stearn ______ (can) not ______ (get) to the examination centre on time.
i) "I ______ only ______ (make) a suggestion!" ______ (shout) John's mother.
j) Students ______ (line up) for their enrolment forms when the university librarian ______ (make) an announcement to evacuate the building immediately.

ACHTUNG

Signalwort für das past progressive *ist* **while,** *für das* simple past *hingegen* **when.**

Simple past, past perfect and past perfect progressive.

5. *Write complete sentences with the ideas below. Put the verbs in the correct past tense. Use the following linking words where necessary to help you join sentences: although, but, and, since, when. Remember to insert articles (a, an, the) where needed.*

- Harry *join* parachuting club in 2002/never *set foot* in airplane before that
- finally *decide* to face his fears instead of running away from them.
- Since he *breaks* his collar bone in a rugby game in 2000, *give up* sports and *spend* too much time alone
- friend James *suggest* the whole idea of parachuting. Before the accident, Harry always *talk* about some day being able to fly like a bird
- Harry *refuse* at first
- James *insist* it would do him good, get him out of his shell
- *beg* Harry to at least give it a try
- his friend *try* to convince him for a long time using every tactic possible
- was thrilled when Harry eventually *give in*
- for almost three years he *jump* (another word for parachuting) every chance he could get
- parachuting *become* Harry's passion. Whenever he *go up* he *feel* exhilarated.

6. *Present perfect or simple past? Fill in the gaps.*

a) Britney Spears _____ (become) one of the most successful singers of our times.
b) In 2006 Kanye West _____ (win) three Grammys for Best Rap-Song, Best Rap-Album and Best Rap-Performance.
c) Robbie Williams _____ (begin) his career in the boy group Take That.
d) Shakira _____ (nominated) in the category 'First Lady' in the 2006 Italian MTV awards.
e) In 2004 the Hollywood Film Festival _____ (honour) Leonardo di Caprio with the Actor of the Year Award for his role in the film The Aviator.
f) Xavier Naidoo, who _____ (belong) to the most successful German group in recent years, _____ (sing) in a boys choir when he _____ (be) a child.
g) Since Xavier also _____ (embark) on a solo career, he _____ (sell) millions of albums.
h) In March 2006 Michael Jackson _____ (sell) most of the animals of his Neverland Ranch.

7. *When Lindsey Hedley, 18, was told she looked like Britney, she made the most of it. She tells CosmoGIRL! how looking like the star could earn her loads. Read her newspaper article.*

"I get paid to be Britney!"

Ever since Britney's first single has come out people have said I look like her. Once, on a flight, the air hostesses whispered about me so much I got upset. They came and apologised to me afterwards, explaining they were convinced I was her. I wouldn't have minded but I was from Newcastle and I was travelling in economy class.

I joined a lookalike agency, Splitting images, after my mum sent in some photos of me. Then I got a call to do a TV show called Stars And Their Doubles. It was nerve-wracking being on TV. Everyone else was so into their characters and I was feeling a bit out of place because I was acting like me, not Britney. There's also one big difference between me and Britney – I can't sing at all! After that I have done a photoshoot for a national newspaper, which I loved. The photographer wanted me to pose just like Britney does in the Slave 4 you video, with my hands all over my body! Strangers in the street shout 'Britney!' at me, too. At first I took it as a compliment, but then people started calling me a wannabe. That's totally unfair – I always looked like that!

8. *In the text there are four highlighted tense mistakes. Look at each sentence carefully and correct the mistakes. Can you also explain the necessary changes?*

Modal auxiliaries sind Verben, die nicht allein stehen können, sondern immer vor dem Infinitiv eines Vollverbs erscheinen. Sie erweitern dessen Bedeutung, indem sie eine Fähigkeit, eine Möglichkeit, eine Bitte oder Aufforderung zum Ausdruck bringen. *Modal auxiliaries* bilden nur ein oder zwei Zeiten, ansonsten werden ihre Ersatzformen *(substitutes)* benutzt. Die folgende Liste gibt einen groben Überblick über die modalen Hilfsverben, ihre Ersatzformen und Verwendungen:

Hilfsverb	**Ersatzform**	**Verwendung zum Ausdruck von**	**Beispiel**
can/cannot	(not) be able to	Fähigkeit, Möglichkeit, Erlaubnis, Bitte	I can sing well.
could (not)	(not) be allowed to	Fähigkeit, Möglichkeit, Erlaubnis in der Vergangenheit; Bitte	He could do that when he was little but I was never allowed to.
may (not)	(not) be allowed to	Bitte um Erlaubnis, Möglichkeit	You weren't allowed to come in then but you may come in now.
might (not)		Möglichkeit, dass etwas geschieht	There might be rain tomorrow.
must (needn't)	(not) have to	Vorschrift, Notwendigkeit, Aufforderung	A year ago she didn't have to work but now she must earn her own money.
mustn't	not be allowed to	Verbot	You mustn't smoke in here! It's prohibited!
ought (not) to		(warnender) Ratschlag, Ermahnung	He ought to call a lawyer.
shall		Vorschlag, Angebot	Shall we go out tonight?
should (not)		Ratschlag	I think you should apologize.
will (won't)	(not) be willing to	höfliche Bitte oder Angebot	Will you please help me?
would (not)	(not) want to refuse to	höfliche Bitte oder Weigerung in der Vergangenheit	Would you pass me the butter, please? They wouldn't let me in the disco.

1. *Body Art has become increasingly popular over the past few years. More and more young people have piercings or tattoos because it makes them look "cool". It is important, however, to take certain precautions.*
Your best friend has decided to have her lip pierced. Can you give her some advice? Use the ideas below and the following modal auxiliaries or their substitutes: should, must, mustn't, have to, can, could, may, might. Convince your friend of the importance of safety measures.

a) your shots/vaccinations up to date, especially for tetanus and hepatitis/save you trouble later on
b) shop around before deciding on a piercing shop
c) ensure piercer is qualified and experienced/check his/her portfolio/piercer wears gloves
d) shop needs to be clean, safe and professional (an autoclave for sterilizing needles and other equipment is available)
e) if the area to be pierced not cleaned with the proper soap (antiseptic), lead to infection
f) the needle used is sterilized and clean

g) piece of jewellery sterilized before attached to body part
h) pierced area is cleaned
i) piercer gives specific instructions for post piercing care
j) know what steps to take if pierced area gets infected; perhaps this sounds too much, but all for your own good.

2. *Teenagers 50 years ago. Answer these questions about adolescents using the past tense. Look at the pictures to get some ideas.*

a) *What did they have to do every day?*
b) *What were they allowed to do at weekends?*
c) *What weren't they allowed to do every day?*
d) *What weren't they able to do?*

3. *Life of teenagers in 50 years. What will they be able to, allowed to and have to do in the future? What not? Write at least 6 sentences.*

Gerunds

Das Gerundium wird auch *ing*-Form genannt, denn es besteht aus dem Infinitiv (Grundform des Verbs) + *-ing*. Oft ist das Gerundium Subjekt oder Objekt des Satzes. Verben, die auf eine Präposition folgen, stehen immer im Gerundium.

*I'm **good at** do**ing** maths.*
*She likes swimm**ing**.*

Das Gerundium wird nach bestimmten Verben, Nomen, Adjektiven und sonstigen Ausdrücken gebraucht. Dazu gehören:

- Verben (+ Präposition): *avoid, consider, enjoy, finish, mind, dream of, feel like, give up, insist on, look forward to, talk about, think about*
- Nomen + Präposition: *chance of, danger of, difficulty in, hope of, interest in, possibility of, reason for, surprise at, way of*
- Adjektiv (+ Präposition): *afraid of, bad at, famous for, fond of, good at, interested in, keen on, proud of, tired of, used to*
- bestimmte Ausdrücke: *it's no use, it's worthwhile, can't help, how about, what about*

Infinitives

Der **Infinitiv mit *to*** steht nach Verben, die einen Ratschlag, eine Erlaubnis, einen Wunsch, eine Warnung oder ein Verbot ausdrücken, z. B. *ask, advise, allow, expect, order, permit, tell, want, warn, wish.* Außerdem steht er nach Adjektiven und ihren Steigerungsformen, nach *the first, second, ...*, nach Fragewörtern sowie nach *whether*.

*She **asked** us **to make** our beds.*
*It is **difficult to find** a good babysitter.*
*He was **the first to cross** the Atlantic in such a small boat.*
*I can show you **where to go**.*

Der **Infinitiv ohne *to*** steht nach Verben der Wahrnehmung und Verben, die eine Beobachtung ausdrücken. Darüber hinaus steht er nach fast allen modalen Hilfsverben und nach *make s.o.* sowie *let:*

*Steven **saw** five children **come** in and **play** their instrument.*
*He **should wear** his hair long, it looks better that way.*
*You really **make me feel** good!*

ACHTUNG

Bei folgenden Verben gibt es keinen Bedeutungsunterschied, wenn man ein Gerundium oder einen Infinitiv anschließt: *begin, start, continue, like, love, hate, intend, prefer.*

It **started to rain**./It **started raining**.

Bei folgenden Verben hingegen gibt es Bedeutungsunterschiede: *stop, forget, mean, regret, remember.*

stop + gerund ➠ eine vergangene Handlung ist vorbei: *It stopped raining.*
stop + infinitive ➠ eine Handlung soll begonnen werden: *I stopped to see you.*
mean + gerund ➠ stellt eine Wirkung dar: *If you run away, it means losing the game.*
mean + infinitive ➠ steht für einen Plan: *He means to become rich.*

Participles

Das **Partizip Präsens** besteht aus dem Infinitiv plus *-ing*. Es wird häufiger wie ein Adjektiv verwendet (z. B. *caring mother*). Es steht nach folgenden Konstruktionen:

- nach Verben der Wahrnehmung, wenn man betonen möchte, dass jemand eine Handlung beobachtet hat: *see, hear, watch, notice, smell, feel* (s. auch Erklärung zu Infinitiv ohne *to*)
  *A few people **watched** the police **arriving** at the crime scene.*
- nach Verben der Ruhe oder Bewegung, wenn man beschreiben möchte, dass zwei Dinge zeitgleich passieren: *come, go, leave, lie, remain, stay*
  *The teacher **left** the class **running** downstairs.*
- nach *keep, find, send*
  *She **kept making** that mistake time and again.*
- nach Konjunktionen wie *after, before, since, when, while*
  ***After finishing** the test, she went home.*

Das **Partizip Perfekt** *(past participle)* besteht bei regelmäßigen Verben aus dem Infinitiv und *-ed* (unregelmäßige Formen muss man lernen). Es wird oft wie ein Adjektiv verwendet *(a parked car)*. Es kann aber auch anstelle eines Relativsatzes stehen oder adverbiale Nebensätze verkürzen:

*Cars **parked** in this zone will be towed. (= Cars that are parked ...)*
***Annoyed** by the music, they left the party. (= Since they were annoyed by ...)*

1. *You have a part-time summer job in a restaurant as a waiter or waitress. Here is a list of the rules for temporary part-time employees.*
Put the verbs in the correct form of the gerund or infinitive. In some cases you will have to use the infinitive without "to".

a) Try ______ at work on time. If you can't avoid ______ late, please ______ me as soon as possible. (arrive/be/call)

b) Remember ______ your apron at all times and ______ your hair out of your face. (wear/keep)

c) After ______ upon arrival, ______ your order pad and purse from my office. (sign in/pick up)

d) Don't be afraid of ______ customers ______ the daily specials. (encourage/order)

e) Before ______ food orders to the kitchen, ______ with customers that you have got things right. (take/check)

f) Let customers ______ at their leisure. ______ them through their meal is simply not our style. (eat/hurry)

g) If you overhear anyone ______ the food, let me ______ immediately. (criticize/know)

h) It is important that you ______ bills prior to ______ customers ______ them. (verify/have/pay)

i) __________ tips is allowed. However, please remember __________ them in the box so we can __________ them up amongst all the employees at the end of the week. (accept/put/divide)

j) Lastly, never forget that we are interested in __________ our customers so they keep __________. Therefore, __________ friendliness and courtesy at all times. (satisfy/come back/show)

2. *Gerund or infinitive? – In some cases the infinitive construction without "to" can be used.*

A lot of teenagers enjoy __________ (spend) time at raves, all night dance parties combined with choreographed laser shows. Although the majority of parents are reluctant __________ (allow) their children __________ (attend) these events, they find it hard __________ (stop) them. Their arguments fall on deaf ears since peer pressure and __________ (be) cool carry more weight with most teenagers.

__________ (gyrate) to the sounds of techno, trance or drum'n'bass is sadly not the only thing that attracts so many of today's youth to this form of entertainment. At raves drug dealers are known for __________ (distribute) "pocket money" club drugs such as ecstasy, LSD (lysergic acid diethylamide), GHB (gamma-hydroxybutyrate) and ketamine to young dancegoers. According to experienced ravers, club drug consumption helps __________ (enhance) the stimulation or "high" they get from the event and is considered __________ (not be) harmful when used responsibly.

__________ (take) these types of drugs, however, is far from harmless. Often the drugs are mixed with other chemicals and substances, can __________ (become) highly addictive and __________ (lead) to overdoses. In fact a high number of overdoses have occurred while __________ (club). Recently strong action has been taken __________ (inform) young people, parents and educators on the dangers of club drug use and __________ (enforce) legal requirements for organized rave events. Parents should __________ (know) at all times what their children are doing, where they are and who they are with. By __________ (curtail) rave activity there is a greater chance of __________ (curb) drug abuse amongst teenagers. It is certainly time __________ (end) this kind of teenage exploitation.

Vocabulary:
apron – Schürze
reluctant – unwillig, widerwillig
gyrate – rotieren, sich drehen
addictive – süchtig machend
curb – zügeln, bändigen

3. *Fill in the blanks with the present participle or past participle form of the verb.*

a) ______ (grin), John waved his medal in the air.
b) The hotel guests were still ______ (frighten) even after the bomb threat was called off.
c) ______ (hide) behind a door, the little girl felt safe from the loud party guests.
d) We saw him ______ (tear) the brand new book.
e) The lawyer felt his client's ______ (speak) word was as valid as a ______ (write) statement.
f) ______ (struggle) to reach the shore, the swimmer ploughed on with as much strength as he could muster.
g) The boy's mother came ______ (scream) out of her home when she heard the news of her son's death.
h) Several victims in the recent bomb attacks were ______ (stick) between the seats of the bus and failed to escape on time.
i) The last two passengers ______ (wait) to board the flight appeared rather suspicious.
j) ______ (drive) by jealousy, Mary slapped Vera on the cheek.

4. *Combine the two sentences using a participle.*

a) I saw a little girl. She was playing with her dog.
b) Robert had read his girlfriend's e-mail. He phoned to thank her for the good advice she had given him.
c) I heard my teacher. He was talking about an idea for a new project.
d) Sarah came home. She opened all the windows because of a terrible smell inside the rooms.
e) The politician was asked to resign because of his affair with a prostitute. He refused.
f) Janet saw the new CD of her favourite singer in the shop. She decided to buy it immediately.
g) Susan ran to the bus stop. She was talking to her friend on her cellphone to tell her she would be late.
h) Anne told her employer she would work overtime – if they gave her the chance to lead the advertising campaign.
i) Nicole Kidman is reputed to be a famous actress. She is Australian.
j) I read the book *"Junk"*. It was written by Melvin Burgess.

5. *Translate the following sentences using participles.*

a) Ich habe in den Ferien einen interessanten amerikanischen Jungen kennen gelernt, der zurzeit in Berlin wohnt.

b) Ich habe ihn auf einer Party getroffen, die sein deutscher Gastbruder gegeben hat.

c) Ich habe die beiden über Joshs Austauschjahr in Deutschland reden hören.

d) Er kam nach Deutschland, um mehr Deutsch und über unsere Kultur zu lernen.

e) Als er auf dem Flughafen in München ankam, hatte er das Gefühl, er würde die Deutschen niemals verstehen.

f) Er beobachtete eine Gruppe von Bayern, die sich über etwas unterhielten, was er nicht verstehen konnte.

g) Josh blieb eine Weile stehen und dachte daran, sofort wieder nach Hause zu fliegen.

h) Er blieb in Deutschland, lernte die Sprache und kann sie jetzt schon sehr gut sprechen.

i) Obwohl er hier viele Freunde gefunden hat, freut er sich schon darauf, wieder in seine Heimat zurückzukehren.

j) Als er seine Gastfamilie fragte, ob sie ihn in den USA besuchen wollten, sagten sie ohne Zögern zu.

Adjectives – Adverbs

Adjektive verwendet man, um zu beschreiben, wie jemand oder etwas ist.
*He is a **perfect** friend. It was a **wonderful** day.*

Adverbien werden häufig verwendet, um zu beschreiben, wie jemand etwas tut. Es gibt aber auch Adverbien, die sich z. B. auf andere Adjektive, Adverbien oder ganze Sätze beziehen können.
*He drives his new car **carefully**.*
*He is a **very** good driver. **Actually**, he has never had an accident.*

Viele Adverbien der Art und Weise werden gebildet, indem man an das Adjektiv die Endung *-ly* anhängt, z. B. *bad – badly, slow – slowly.*

Die Grundform von Adjektiven und Adverbien heißt „Positiv". Wenn man Personen, Dinge, Zustände oder Tätigkeiten miteinander vergleicht, steigert man Adjektive und Adverbien, um Gleichheit oder Ungleichheit auszudrücken. Einsilbige Adjektive und Adverbien oder zweisilbige Adjektive, die auf *-er, -le, -ow, -y* enden, werden mit *-er* (Komparativ) und *-est* (Superlativ) gesteigert, z. B. *nice – nicer – nicest, friendly – friendlier – friendliest.*
Alle anderen zwei- und mehrsilbigen Adjektive und Adverbien werden mit ***more*** und ***most*** gesteigert:
beautiful – more beautiful – most beautiful
beautifully – more beautifully – most beautifully

Um **Gleichheit** auszudrücken, kann man ***as*** **– Positiv –** ***as*** verwenden, z. B. *as cold as ice.*
Um **Ungleichheit** auszudrücken, kann man ***not as*** **– Positiv –** ***as*** oder **Komparativ +** ***than*** verwenden:
not as cold as ice, not as beautiful as …
colder than ice, more beautiful than …

Satzstellung von Adverbien
Je nachdem, auf welchen Satzteil sich Adverbien beziehen, stehen sie an verschiedenen Stellen innerhalb des Satzes. Sie stehen im Englischen jedoch niemals zwischen Verb und direktem Objekt: *He* ***often*** *buys new CDs.* (nicht ➠ He buys often new CDs.)
Satzadverbien stehen am Satzanfang: ***Fortunately****, we haven't had any problems.*
Adverbien der Art und Weise stehen meist hinter dem Verb oder dessen Objekt, also am Satzende: *He came home* ***happily****.*
Häufigkeitsadverbien stehen nach dem (ersten) Hilfsverb bzw. vor dem Vollverb: *We have* ***never*** *been to London.* Aber nach einer Form von *be*, z. B. *He is* ***often*** *late.*
Folgen mehrere adverbiale Bestimmungen aufeinander, so stehen sie in dieser Reihenfolge:
Art und Weise – Ort – Zeit:
She walks ***slowly home in the afternoon****.*

1. *Put the adjectives and adverbs in the suitable form of the comparative or superlative.*

a) (modern) In Canada the majority of high school students attend ________ comprehensive schools than those existing in Germany.
b) (good) ________ special needs programmes to assist weak students, high achievers, EFL language learners and even the handicapped etc. form an integral part of the curriculum.
c) (much) Unlike in Germany, students are not streamed after grade four. In Canada, they are given ________ time to decide.
d) (little) ________ pressure is placed on young learners to perform academically at such an early stage of their school career.
e) (bad) German schools are certainly not ________ than Canadian ones – two countries, two systems.
f) (easy) (good) However, Canadian working parents find it ________ than their German counterparts to organize child care. This is due to full day schools as well as ________ supervised after school activities in Canada.

g) (extreme) (high) It is ________ difficult for both parents to work in Germany. Classes generally end before lunch and places in after school centres (Hort) are ________ coveted.

h) (good) (successful) Which is the ________ school system of the two? A combination of both would probably be ________.

i) (slow) When it comes to education, progress is often ________ than one expects.

j) (important) (needed) The ________ thing is to realize when reforms are ________ and to ensure that pupils or students do not suffer from too much experimentation.

2. *Place the adverbs or adverbial phrases in the correct position in the sentences.*

a) (mostly) In high school, overall grades are based on continual assessment.

b) (generally) Students receive what is known as credits for subjects passed at the end of the year.

c) (at the end of grade twelve) In order to graduate from high school, one has to accumulate the required number of credits.

d) (until now) University entrance grade requirements have varied depending on the course of study to be pursued.

e) (moreover) We do not have secondary school state exams equivalent to the "Realschulabschluss" or "Abitur," unlike the English with their nationwide O-levels (GCSE) and A-levels (advanced levels).

f) (seldom) High school students in Germany are given a second chance to rewrite final examinations which they fail.

g) (unfortunately) Canadian tertiary institutions have higher tuition costs than German ones.

h) (successfully) Students who have completed grade twelve can enter community college, polytechnic institutions or university.

i) (in Germany) (often) (at the age of 10) School children are placed under enormous pressure.

3. *Translate into English, please. Pay attention to the correct position of the adverbs.*

a) Verschiedene PISA-Studien zeigen, dass deutsche Schüler nicht so gute Ergebnisse haben wie Schüler anderer europäischer Länder.
b) Leider schließen nicht alle Schüler die Schule erfolgreich ab.
c) Man findet oft mehr motivierte Schüler an moderneren und besser ausgerüsteten Schulen.
d) Dringend benötigte Reformen des Schulsystems werden in Deutschland nur langsam durchgesetzt.

Einfache Aussagesätze werden im Englischen nach einem festen Muster zusammengesetzt: Subjekt – Verb – restlicher Satz. Dieses Muster verändert sich auch nicht, wenn dem Satz ein Nebensatz oder eine adverbiale Bestimmung vorangeht (bei mehreren aufeinander folgenden adverbialen Bestimmungen ➠ siehe Satzstellung bei Adverbien).

Nebensatz	Subjekt	Verb	restlicher Satz
	Katharine	*loves*	*sports.*
When school was over	*my teacher*	*heard*	*all the children leaving.*

Verneinte Sätze bildet man, indem man vor das Verb ein verneintes Hilfsverb stellt. Gibt es kein Hilfsverb in der Aussage, wird *don't/doesn't* oder *didn't* eingefügt.

Subjekt	vern. Hilfsverb	Verb	restlicher Satz
Nick	*didn't*	*enjoy*	*the match.*
Tuan	*hasn't*	*seen*	*his latest film.*

Fragen bildet man mit Hilfe eines Hilfsverbs, außer wenn nach dem Subjekt des Satzes gefragt wird. In Sätzen ohne Hilfsverb wird *do/does/did* verwendet. Wenn aber nach dem Subjekt eines Satzes gefragt wird, ist die Wortstellung „Fragewort – Verb – restlicher Satz".

Fragewort	Hilfsverb	Subjekt	Verb	restlicher Satz
	Can	*you*	*speak*	*English?*
Where	*did*	*he*	*go*	*last night?*
Who			*helped*	*my daughter?*

1. *Find the correct order of the words and phrases to form sentences.*

a) the supermarket – in the evening – goes to – never – Ben
b) reading – spends – Kevin – often – a book – his afternoons – in the park
c) this wonderful town – has been living – now – Jenny – for – in – more than 12 years
d) went to – the new film – Alan – after – had seen – bed – he
e) the meeting – although – was – came to – Frank – ill – terribly – he
f) because – I – wanted to – phoned – where – the concert – my friend – was held – know – I
g) the new Spielberg film – the cinema – went to – see – they – in order to
h) was surfing – with our dog – I – my parents – the net – were taking a walk – while
i) fascinating – such – ever – you – have – seen – show – a?
j) the jacket – buy – where – did – I – so much – which – you – like?

2. *The Millers, a family of four with their son Alec and their daughter Kate, were on holiday in Spain. Ask as many questions as possible. Add any words you consider useful/necessary.*

Who Where When What Why How (much/often/long)	did (not)	the Millers Mr Miller Mrs Miller Alec Kate	go to ... eat/drink ... talk to ... spend ... play with ... do ... see ... arrive/leave stay	?

Conjunctions

Konjunktionen verbinden Satzteile miteinander und deuten eine Beziehung zwischen ihnen an. Je nachdem, welche Beziehung die Satzteile zueinander haben, werden unterschiedliche Konjunktionen verwendet. Die folgende Tabelle gibt eine Übersicht über verschiedene Satztypen und ihre möglichen Konjunktionen:

Type of clause	Possible conjunctions	Example
time	*when, whenever, before, since, after, until, for*	*She worked all day* ***until*** *she was really tired.*
conditional	*if, unless, as long as*	*You can come in* ***as long as*** *you are quiet.*
purpose	*in order to, so that*	*He left home* ***in order to*** *buy some food.*
reason	*because, since, as*	*I love you* ***because*** *you're pretty.*
result	*so that*	*I gave her the money* ***so that*** *she could pay for the taxi.*
concessive	*although, though, while, however, in spite of, despite*	*I knew he wouldn't come to the party* ***although*** *I had invited him several times.*
place	*where, wherever*	*He will follow me* ***wherever*** *I go.*
manner	*as, like*	*He was very friendly* ***like*** *a good colleague.*

1. *Complete the sentences.*

a) You can phone and ask me for help *whenever* ...

b) She won't be able to solve the problem *unless* ...

c) He had always supported her *although* ...

d) My friends were playing computer games *while* ...

e) We will order some vegetarian pizzas *if* ...

f) She switched on the TV *in order to* ...

g) He realized what mistake he had made *when* ...

h) I left a message for you *as* ...

i) It was the first time I'd met him *since* ...

j) Her parents support her financially *so that* ...

Prepositions

Präpositionen sind Wörter zur Ortsbestimmung wie ***on, in, at, to, about, with, of*** und ***for***. Oft ist es so, dass einzelne Präpositionen mit speziellen Verben zusammen verwendet werden, deren Bedeutung sich dadurch verändert.

EXAMPLE *Someday, I want to be* ***on*** *television. (I want to appear on a television show.)*
Someday, I want to be ***in*** *television. (I want to work in the television industry.)*
Turn ***on*** *the TV.*
Turn ***off*** *the TV.*

Außerdem können Präpositionen eine Richtung angeben, z. B. ***to, toward, on, onto, in, through*** oder ***into***.

1. *Complete the following sentences with the correct preposition:* to, toward, on, onto, in, *or* into. *Some sentences may have more than one possible correct answer. Remember that a few verbs of motion take only* on *rather than* onto.

a) Alice has returned ______ her home town.

b) The dog leaped ______ the lake.

c) Are the girls still going ______ the pool?

d) Alexander slipped ______ the floor.

e) The train drove ______ the station.

f) We walked ______ the school, but turned back before we reached it.

g) The children were climbing ______ the monkey bars.

h) Lucas got ______ Tom's car and turned ______ the radio.

i) I called to the man on the bridge, "Hang ______, we're coming!"

j) Just called ______ say I love you.

k) Nelson apologized for interrupting me, and told me to carry ______ talking.

2. *Complete the following sentences with the correct preposition:* in, at, beside, between, under, over *and* on.

a) Will you please wait for me ______ the bus stop?

b) The book is ______ the magazines.

c) The dog was ______ the table waiting for someone to slip him a treat.

d) The last time I saw Harriet, she was ______ the carnival.

e) I wanted to sit down, but there wasn't a chair to sit ______.

f) When my cousin was unemployed, he used to say he was ______ jobs.

g) He climbed ______ the fence and into the neighbour's yard.

Relative Clauses

Relativsätze sind Nebensätze, die sich auf ein Nomen im Hauptsatz beziehen. Man unterscheidet zwischen zwei Arten:

Notwendige Relativsätze *(defining relative clauses)* enthalten wichtige Informationen, ohne die der Hauptsatz allein nicht verständlich wäre. Sie beziehen sich auf das Wort, das sie näher beschreiben und werden nicht durch Kommas vom Hauptsatz getrennt.
Kevin is a boy ***who loves nature****.*
This is one of the flower pots ***that should be watered****.*
A horn is the object in a car ***which*** *makes a warning noise when you press it.*
Die Relativpronomen *(relative pronouns)* können Subjekt oder Objekt des Nebensatzes sein. Für Personen verwendet man *who, that* und *whose*, für Sachen *which, that* und *whose*.
Relativpronomen können auch weggelassen werden, wenn sie das Objekt eines notwendigen Relativsatzes sind. Solche Satzkonstruktionen nennt man ***contact clause***.
The girl who/that I had seen was black. ➡ *The girl I had seen was black.*
The book that you gave me was interesting. ➡ *The book you gave me ...*

Nicht notwendige Relativsätze *(non-defining relative clauses)* werden fast nur im formellen Englisch verwendet. Sie enthalten Informationen, die nicht unbedingt zum Verständnis des Hauptsatzes erforderlich sind, und werden durch Kommas vom Hauptsatz getrennt.

J. K. Rowling, who is the author of Harry Potter, is one of the richest women in the UK.
My town, which was founded in 1260, is very picturesque.

Für Personen verwendet man *who* oder *whom*, für Sachen *which*, jedoch niemals *that*.

1. *Combine the two sentences using a relative pronoun without changing their meaning. Omit the pronoun where possible to form a contact clause. Make any other necessary changes.*

a) My sister and I went to see the new Star Wars film. It was one of the best films she had seen this year.
b) Susan would really like to go to the Britney Spears concert. It will be in Munich.
c) The school books were scattered on the floor. They belonged to Milton.
d) In-line skating is a great way to keep fit. It helps to strengthen your muscles.
e) My mother is always complaining about the amount of time I spend on the telephone. She also carries on long phone conversations with her friends.
f) Bullying is a serious problem in many schools. We have been having class discussions on bullying.
g) Roald Dahl wrote *Charlie and the Chocolate Factory*. His books are appreciated by both adults and children.
h) Employment Services of Disneyland, California made a part time job offer to one of the students in our class. It was Paul Kramer.
i) I am reading a book. It is called *Harry Potter and the Half-Blood Prince*.
j) David Beckham has a cool hairstyle. I like it a lot.

2. *Some sentences are correct and some not. Correct the mistakes where necessary and tick the sentences with no mistakes.*

a) The English course what John applied for takes place in Kent, England.
b) The lady which came into the restaurant ordered a lunch special.
c) He will get the exam grade he wanted.
d) He told me a story what I had already heard.
e) They were the last group that handed in their History assignment.
f) Their Geography teacher to who they sent a letter lives in a very remote area.
g) Anorexia, which is big problem amongst teenagers, can lead to severe physical and emotional damage.
h) Sandra, who her sister has been an avid supporter and member of *Amnesty International,* has just landed a job with their London branch.
i) Pollution in urban areas, what has become an increasingly growing concern, must be reduced.
j) Jenny was named School Council President, which is quite an honour.

3. *Translate into English.*

a) Wir können die Eintrittskarten, die ich gestern bestellt habe, heute Abend abholen.
b) Ich habe eine Filmkritik über den Film, von dem du erzählt hast, in der Zeitung gelesen.
c) Jodie Foster, die die Hauptrolle in *Flightplan* spielt, war im Herbst in Berlin.
d) Sie spielt die Rolle als Mutter eines Kinds, das im Flugzeug spurlos verschwunden ist, sehr gut.
e) Es gibt Leute, die gehen nur ins Kino, um ihre Lieblingsschauspieler zu sehen.
f) Wir haben in unserer Stadt überhaupt kein Kino, was jammerschade ist.

Conditional Sentences

Bedingungssätze bestehen aus einem Hauptsatz und einem *if*-Satz (in beliebiger Reihenfolge). Man drückt damit aus, was unter bestimmten Bedingungen geschieht, geschehen könnte oder geschehen wäre. Man unterscheidet drei Typen von Bedingungssätzen:

Typ I: Erfüllbare Bedingung
Wenn eine Bedingung realistisch und erfüllbar ist, benutzt man im *if-clause* das *simple present*, im Hauptsatz das *will*-Futur:
If I do *my homework every day,* *I* ***will pass*** *the test.*
He ***will go*** *to the dance lesson* ***if*** *you* ***join*** *him.*

Typ II: Unwahrscheinliche oder nicht erfüllbare Bedingung
Wenn eine Bedingung unrealistisch ist oder nicht den Tatsachen entspricht, benutzt man im *if-clause* das *simple past*, im Hauptsatz das *conditional:*
If *you* ***weren't*** *so mean all the time,* *I* ***would help*** *you.*
She ***would buy*** *more clothes* ***if*** *she* ***had*** *the money.*

Typ III: Unmögliche Bedingung
Diesen Typ verwendet man, wenn eine Bedingung nicht erfüllt werden kann, weil sie sich auf die Vergangenheit bezieht. Im *if-clause* steht das *past perfect*, im Hauptsatz das *conditional perfect:*
If *I* ***had known*** *you then,* *I* ***would have married*** *you.*
We ***wouldn't have had*** *cramps* ***if*** *we* ***hadn't eaten*** *so much.*

ACHTUNG

Ein Komma benutzt man nur, wenn man mit dem if-clause *beginnt.*

1. *Match the following sentence halves.*

If my mum has to work this evening,	I would do my maths homework instead.
If I had time this evening,	she would have made a fantastic dinner.
If she wasn't in,	he would spend more time with us.
If mum had come home earlier last night,	I'll have to look after my baby brother.
If she hadn't ordered the pizza,	I'll never forgive him.
If he wants to see me again,	I'll tell him about my new friend.
If dad didn't have to work so much,	he'll phone me, I'm sure.
If he has breakfast with us on Saturday,	I would call my friend.
If he forgets my birthday,	I wouldn't have got to know the handsome pizza man.

2. *Complete the conditional sentences. Pay attention to the correct tenses.*

a) My mum wouldn't complain about my marks at school if I ________ my homework regularly. (do)

b) If I get my driver's licence, I ________ you home every day. (drive)

c) If we ________ by bus instead of using the car all the time, we could do something to save our environment. (go)

d) Some people say there might be another nuclear accident like the one in Tschernobyl if we ________ using nuclear energy. (go on)

e) If I ________ so much about environmental problems, I wouldn't have started sorting our waste some years ago. (not learn)

3. *Complete the missing parts of the sentences below in a sensible manner. Use the conditional types 1 or 2.*

a) If John doesn't play football this season, the school team ________ championships.

b) More members would show up to our photography club meetings if we ________.

c) I won't be angry if you ________.

d) If drug dealers didn't exploit teenagers at clubs, they ________.

e) Writing letters the old-fashioned way may become obsolete if ________ e-mails instead.

f) The orchestra wouldn't know how fast to play a piece if the conductor ________.

g) Computer technology will expand even more if progress ________.

h) Would you please help me if you ________ some time?

i) "Olivia and Raphael, you may not go swimming if you both ________ fighting right now!"

j) "Do you think Sam would go to the dance with me if I ________?"

Reported Speech (Indirect Speech)

Man verwendet die **indirekte Rede**, um zu berichten, was jemand gesagt oder geschrieben hat. Da sich die Sprecherperspektive ändert, müssen bei einem Text, der von direkter in indirekte Rede verändert wird, einige Änderungen vorgenommen werden, z. B. Pronomen und Possessivbegleiter, Adverbialbestimmungen und vor allem Tempora. Die Zeiten der direkten Rede werden in der indirekten um eine Zeitstufe in die Vergangenheit verschoben (siehe Tabelle, *backshift of tenses*). In der Umgangssprache werden allerdings *simple past* oder *past progressive* häufig in der indirekten Rede beibehalten.

Aussagesätze werden in der indirekten Rede mit Verben eingeleitet wie z. B. *agree, answer, know, point out, remark, say, tell s. o., think* etc.
Nick: "John is my best friend!" ➟ *Nick said (that) John was his best friend.*
May: "I will travel to Florida." ➟ *May told us (that) she would travel to Florida.*

Fragesätze werden in der indirekten Rede mit Verben wie *ask, want to know, wonder* etc. eingeleitet. Wenn die direkte Rede mit einem Fragewort beginnt, wird dieses auch in der indirekten Rede übernommen. Bei Fragen ohne Fragewort verwendet man *if* oder *whether*.
David: "What do you like to eat?" ➟ *David asked what she liked to eat.*
David: "Do you like peas?" ➟ *David asked whether she liked peas.*

TIPP

Backshift of tenses

Direct Speech	**Reported/Indirect Speech**
simple present	simple past
present progressive	past progressive
present perfect	past perfect
simple past	past perfect
past perfect	--- (past perfect *bleibt*)
will-future	would + infinitive
going-to future	was/were going to + infinitive
can	could
may	might

Zeitangaben der direkten Rede, die am selben Tag, im selben Monat oder Jahr in indirekter Rede wiedergegeben werden, werden übernommen. Wird aber zu einem späteren Zeitpunkt berichtet, verändern sie sich folgendermaßen:

Direct Speech	***Reported/Indirect Speech***
today	*that day*
now	*then*
tomorrow	*the next/following day*
tonight	*that night*
this week/month/year	*that week/month/year*
next week/month/year	*the next/following week/month/year*
last week/year/Saturday	*the week/year/Saturday before*
two days ago	*two days before*

Befehle *(imperatives)*, Bitten oder Ratschläge werden in indirekter Rede mit einem einleitenden Verb wie *ask, forbid, order, persuade, remind, request, tell, warn* etc. eingeleitet. Der Befehl wird durch *should* oder den Infinitiv mit *to* ausgedrückt.
Rita: *"Please, be quiet now!"* ➠ *Rita said they should be quiet.* ➠ *Rita asked them to be quiet.*

1. *Convert the following sentences into reported speech. Start like this: He said ...*

a) I am going to Dublin for the U2 Concert.
b) I am not just seeing the band, I'm helping with the show.
c) I will be helping set up the stage and the light show.
d) It is an amazing thing and I can't believe it is happening to me.
e) I was following the band throughout Europe on their last tour.
f) In just under two weeks, I saw them 10 times in 10 different cities.
g) At every concert, I managed to get front row seats, although sometimes they were really expensive.
h) After the eighth show, Bono told me that he had seen me too many times and that I should join the road crew for the tour.
i) I thought Bono was joking with me, but he was serious.
j) I am still going to University next year, but right now I'm enjoying an experience of a lifetime.

2. *Now convert these questions into reported speech.*

a) Bono, when did you give your first concert?
b) How did U2 become successful in Ireland?
c) Had you ever thought of becoming famous before your success?
d) Have you got enough time for friends despite your job?
e) What are your plans for the next years?
f) Do you think you will still be on stage in 10 years?
g) Can you imagine doing any other job?
h) Have you ever been disappointed after a concert?

3. *Convert these commands and requests of a concerned mother into reported speech.*

a) Don't buy a new CD every week.

b) Tell me when you intend to go to a concert.

c) Don't spend the night with other people you don't know.

d) Take a taxi home if the concert ends very late.

e) Bring me an autograph of my favourite singer.

Das Aktiv hebt hervor, wer oder was eine Handlung vornimmt. Das **Passiv** hingegen hebt hervor, was mit einer Person oder Sache geschieht. Dabei ist meist unwichtig, wer oder was diese Handlung ausführt. Das Passiv lässt sich von allen Verben bilden, die im Aktiv ein direktes Objekt nach sich ziehen (transitive Verben). Es wird mit einer Form von *be* + Partizip Perfekt (dritte Verbform) gebildet.

Right-hand drive Volkswagen cars ***are made*** *in South Africa.*
Coffee and cake ***have been served*** *in the living room.*
Money ***can be exchanged*** *here.*

Bei Verben, die im Aktiv mit einem direkten und einem indirekten Objekt verbunden sind (wie z. B. *ask, give, offer, pay, promise, send, show, teach, tell, write*), wird meistens das **indirekte Objekt als Subjekt des Passivsatzes** verwendet.

Aktiv	dir. Obj.	indir. Obj.		Passiv
Someone gave	*him*	*the key.*	➟	*He was given the key.*
selten:				*The key was given to him.*

Wenn der Handelnde im Passivsatz explizit genannt werden soll, schließt man ihn mit dem so genannten ***by-agent*** an.

The school report was signed ***by the student's parents****.*

Bei Verben mit Präpositionen (z. B. *ask for, laugh at, speak about, talk about, think of*, etc.) folgt die Präposition wie im Aktiv direkt dem Verb.

The children ***talked about*** *the problem.* ➟ *The problem was* ***talked about****.*

1. *Here is a list of some of the school rules at Laura's school. Change them into the passive voice, where possible.*

a) Enter the school by the south doors only. We lock all the other doors until morning classes are over.
b) We do not allow running in the halls.
c) The school secretary keeps a set of keys for all classrooms.
d) Students in charge of extra curricular activities must lock all classrooms before they leave the building.
e) Do not damage school property.
f) You must wear non-marking running shoes in the gym.
g) You should use your lockers for personal belongings.
h) We expect you to be on time for your classes. Latecomers must sign in at the principal's office.
i) If you are late three times, we send a letter to your parents.
j) The school board will suspend any student caught cheating on an exam.
k) If a teacher has given a student a red notice, which is a serious warning, he or she must have his parents sign it.

2. *Kevin is worried about his job interview and talks to his friend Sam who is more experienced. Fill in the blanks with suitable passive constructions. Look for signal words to help you with the tenses.*

EXAMPLE *Kevin: What do you think I should wear for my interview next Monday? Does the way a person dresses influence employers?*
Sam: A jacket and tie, at least. Employers are always influenced by the way a person dresses.

a) Kevin: Will more than one person ask me questions during the interview?
Sam: I'm sure you ______________ (ask) questions by a panel of interviewers.

b) Kevin: What kind of questions can I expect?
Sam: Questions on your family background, schooling, past work experience and general interests ______________ (expect).

c) Kevin: They are interviewing Petra today. We must find out how it goes.
Sam: That's right she ______________ (interview).

d) Kevin: Have they ever conducted more than one interview for such a position?
Sam: Oh yes, more than one interview ______________ (conduct) on several occasions.

e) Kevin: I heard that last year they really put applicants to the test.
Sam: Not just last year, but the year before as well, applicants ______________ (put) through the wringer.

f) Kevin: Did you hear about Jack? Two weeks ago while he ______________ (interview), someone from personnel interrupted and called off the whole thing. Apparently when they double-checked his application form, he hadn't fulfilled all their requirements. I find that unprofessional, don't you?
Sam: I guess so, but some of the employees in personnel ______________ (be put under pressure) and so documents ______________ (not double-check) thoroughly. Rules are rules, though, and requirements ______________ (have to fulfil), otherwise it's not fair to other applicants.

g) Kevin: How about if we do a mock interview and you can tell me what I need to work on?
Sam: Certainly. I'll try my best to tell you what needs ______________ (work on).

Girls and guitars

Stars like Avril Lavigne have made guitars popular with girls, writes Chloe Anthony

The guitar has always been an essential part of any rock or pop group, but the most famous guitar players have always been men. This is changing as more and more young women are playing the guitar.
There have also been famous female guitar players such as Suzi Quatro or the Bangles, but recently the music scene has seen the great success of "girl bands". At the moment, probably the most famous female guitarist is Avril Lavigne, who has inspired many young women to start learning the guitar.
Music experts say there is a general revival of the guitar today. After the heyday of the electric guitar in the sixties, the instrument went out of fashion as techno became the sound of the day. Ten years ago £30 million was spent on guitars in the UK. Last year people in the UK spent £105 million on guitars.
Five years ago in the US, Tish Ciravolo, a bass guitar player, set up the first company to produce guitars made for girls. Daisy Rock guitars are lighter with narrower necks. They come in colours like Peppermint Pink and Awesome Blue and models called Butterfly – Heartbreaker, Stardust and Rock Candy.
Tish says, "What I wanted to do was not only design a guitar for a girl to play, but to change the consciousness – make the sight of a girl playing the guitar as natural as that of a girl playing the flute. And, apart from just designing guitars that girls could play, I believed a guitar should be fun – I wanted them to be girlie – I wanted girls aged eight to 11 to say, 'Wow – I want to play!'"
So you want to play guitar in a band … here are some tips on how to go about it. First you need a decent guitar. Second you have to practise. The best thing to do is to find yourself a teacher. If you can't, or don't have the money to pay for lessons, then you can use a book or just learn to play your favourite songs. Third, you should find a band. Ask friends, create a network, practise in the garage. Lastly, be confident, have an open mind and have fun!

(Source: *Read on*, November Issue 2005, page 5)

1. *Read the text and find examples of the following grammatical structures and mark them in the text. You will need them in exercises 1–5.*
Four different tenses; passive, active; comparative and superlative forms of adjectives; modal auxiliaries; participles; gerund; relative clauses; conditional clauses.

II Tenses

1. *What tenses are used in these sentences and why?*

sentence	*tense*	*why*
Music experts say there is a general revival of the guitar today.		
This is changing as more and more young women are playing the guitar.		
… but recently the music scene has seen the great success of "girl bands".		
Last year people in the UK spent £105 million on guitars.		

2. *Using these tenses, form sentences of your own about music.*

3. *Translate the sentences into English using suitable tenses.*

a) Mein Freund sagt, dass wir eine musikalische Familie sind.
b) Meine Mutter singt wirklich gut und spielt Flöte.
c) Mein Vater begann Geige zu spielen, als er fünf Jahre alt war, sodass er das sehr gut kann.
d) Ich spiele seit zwei Jahren Gitarre.
e) Zurzeit nehme ich Klavierunterricht.
f) Nächsten Monat wird meine 6-jährige Schwester Mitglied im Chor werden.

III Active and Passive

1. *Find an example of the active and another one of the passive in the same paragraph of the text "Girls and Guitars" (p. 101) and write down how the passive is formed.*

active	***passive***

2. *Use the prompts below to form passive sentences.*

a) Bob Dylan – regard – one of the most important musicians of rock and pop music
b) famous songs like "Knockin' On Heaven's Door" and "Like A Rolling Stone" – write – Bob Dylan
c) "Blowin' In The Wind" – one of his first hits – write – in the 1960s
d) first rock double album "Blonde On Blonde" – release – 1966
e) song "Hurricane" from the album Desire – record – 1975 – release – 1976
f) other singers and musicians like REM, U2 and Sheryl Crow – influence – by him
g) at the beginning of the 21st century – award – Oscar – for his composition "Things Have Changed"
h) surely – his songs – hear, play, sing – in the future

IV Adjectives

1. *Complete the chart with the help of the text "Girls and Guitars". Write down two ways of how we compare adjectives.*

positive	***comparative***	***superlative***
famous	more famous	
light		lightest
narrow		narrowest
good	better	

2. *Compare the given items.*

a) a local politician – the German chancellor – the US President (powerful)
b) a gramophone – a record player – a CD-player (modern)
c) an autograph – an interview – a live concert (interesting)
d) a crossword puzzle – a test – an exam (difficult)

V Modal auxiliaries

1. *Find sentences with three different modal auxiliaries or their substitutes in the text "Girls and Guitars".*

2. *Complete the chart.*

modal auxiliaries	***substitutes***
	be able to
	be allowed to
must	

3. *Fill in the gaps using modal auxiliaries and their substitutes.*

a) As a child I ______ go to concerts of my favourite bands.
b) But since I liked music a lot, I ______ play simple songs on the guitar at the age of eight.
c) In order to learn how to play more musical instruments I ______ attend music school twice a week.
d) Today I ______ only play five different instruments, I also have my own band.

TEST: GRAMMATIK

VI Besondere Verbformen: Infinitives, Gerunds, Participles

1. *Read the following sentences and analyse the marked parts in the sentences. Say what forms of the verb they are. Rewrite sentences a) and b) using other structures.*

a) Five years ago in the US, Tish Ciravolo, a bass guitar player, set up the first company to produce guitars made for girls.
b) Tish says, "What I wanted to do was not only design a guitar for a girl to play, but to change the consciousness – make the sight of a girl playing the guitar as natural as that of a girl playing the flute.
c) And, apart from just designing guitars that girls could play, I believed a guitar should be fun – I wanted them to be girlie – I wanted girls aged eight to 11 to say, 'Wow – I want to play!'"

2. *Now rewrite the sentences below using participle constructions.*

a) Last week Britney bought a guitar in a music shop in London. It was offered for £ 160.
b) She had watched the shop assistant. He had shown different flutes to a woman and her child.
c) After she had bought the new instrument she wanted to try it out immediately.
d) At the moment Britney is sitting in her bedroom. She is playing her new guitar.

VII Relative clauses

At the moment, probably the most famous female guitarist is Avril Lavigne, who has inspired many young women to start learning the guitar.

1. *Use relative clauses to explain the following things / terms.*

piano, concert, song, guitarist, orchestra, CD

VIII Conditional clauses

1. *What type of conditional clause is this?*

If you can't, or don't have the money to pay for lessons, then you can use a book or just learn to play your favourite songs.

2. *Put the sentence halves together. Write the correct letter next to each number below. You have to be familiar with all types of conditional sentences for this exercise. Then write down what type of conditional sentence they are.*

1. I would have been heartbroken	A. if I weighed less.
2. If Glen hadn't been ill for two weeks	B. please give him my love.
3. If you visit us in Glasgow	C. if you had left me.
4. I would eat more chocolate	D. he would have had better results.
5. If you meet Danny	E. we will go to the Indian restaurant.

Special report: Teens and Drugs in America

MEGAN HAKEMAN was just 12 years old the first time she tried huffing. She was hanging out with six friends after school, when one of them took out an aerosol can, sprayed it into a towel and breathed it in. "I had no idea what he was doing," says Megan, now 16. "All of a sudden, he got this dazed look on his face, and he passed out." Her friend woke up a few seconds later and easily convinced the rest of the group to give it a try.
"He looked happy," Megan recalls. "So I decided, why not?"

Two months later Megan, who lives in Watertown, South Dakota, was addicted to inhalants. Hooked on the euphoric feeling the chemicals gave her, she was huffing every day after school, either with friends or alone in her room. She'd use Glade air freshener, WD40 spray – anything she could find under the kitchen or bathroom sink.

"Twenty minutes after I huffed, I'd start craving more," she says. "I was never hungry because inhalants became my food."

While Megan believes that a lot of teens start huffing simply because they're bored ("I live in a hick town. Kids huff because they have nothing else to do."), her own addiction came from a desperate need to escape her feelings.

Sexually assaulted by a 17-year-old boy the summer before seventh grade, Megan kept the incident a secret for months out of fear and embarrassment. "My life became really dark," she says. "Huffing was a way to get out of my head. It kind of numbed me."

Even as her pain and addiction worsened, Megan's parents never noticed. "I knew my mom wouldn't know what huffing was," she says. "And it was easy to hide because I was using products from the house."

Inevitably Megan's anguish grew to the point where huffing offered her no relief. Finally, on Halloween night, after a fight with her brother, Megan's pain was more than she could bear. This time, instead of reaching for inhalants (which she didn't know could be lethal) she began swallowing handfuls of Tylenol pills and prescription drugs. "I felt like nothing mattered anymore," she says. "I wanted to die." Just at that moment – luckily for Megan – her mother, Joan, walked into the room. "I wasn't unconscious," she says, "but I was really out of it."

Terrified, Joan rushed her daughter to the emergency room. Once stabilized, a disoriented Megan confessed she was a huffer to a counsellor, who informed her shocked and frightened parents. Days later, afraid for their daughter's life, they checked Megan into Our Home, a treatment center and school for huffers. In daily group-therapy sessions with other teens who had abused inhalants, Megan finally felt the freedom to open up. "We all had used huffing to solve our problems," she says, "so we could really relate to each other."

She's been clean now for more than two years, but Megan admits it hasn't been easy. "When I got back from treatment, a lot of my friends still huffed – even when I was around."

While in treatment Megan told her mom that she ultimately wanted to help other teens with similar problems. "It's more effective if kids hear about huffing from someone their own age," she says. So now she travels the country talking at schools. "I tell them it's not worth ruining your life for a 15-minute high."

(Lori Leibovich in: *Teen People Magazine* 3/2003; copyright time inc.)

Vocabulary:

huff – schnüffeln
aerosol can – Spraydose
dazed – benommen, weggetreten
pass out – in Ohnmacht fallen
hook – hängen an, abhängen von
Glade air freshener, WD40 spray – *(Produktnamen)*
hick town – Provinznest
assault – angreifen
numb – betäuben
anguish – Leiden, Schmerzen
Tylenol® – *(Markenname eines Schmerzmittels)*
prescription drugs – verschreibungspflichtige Medikamente
treatment – Behandlung

ABSCHLUSSTEST

1. *Reported Speech: Rewrite the following paragraphs into reported speech.*

“My life became really dark. Huffing was a way to get out of my head. It kind of numbed me.”
“I knew my mom wouldn’t know what huffing was. And it was easy to hide because I was using products from the house.”
“It’s more effective if kids hear about huffing from someone their own age. I tell them it’s not worth ruining your life for a 15-minute high.”

Start like this:

Megan said ...

2. *Questions: In the text, Megan tells us a lot about her huffing. What – do you think – could have been the reporter’s questions? Form six questions asking about the information Megan gives.*

EXAMPLE *R.: When did you start huffling? M.: “I was just 12 years old ...”*

3. *Tenses: Define and explain the use of the tenses in the following sentences.*

Example	Tense	Explanation
She was hanging out with six friends after school, when one of them took out an aerosol can, sprayed it onto a towel and breathed it. (ll. 1–3)		
Two months later Megan, who lives in Watertown, South Dakota, was addicted to inhalants. (ll. 7–8)		
"We all had used huffing to solve our problems." (ll. 33–34)		
She's been clean now for more than two years, but Megan admits it hasn't been easy. (l. 35)		
"It's more effective if kids hear about huffing from someone their own age." (ll. 38–39)		

4. *Writing:*
a) Write a summary of the text in about 100–150 words.
b) "... it's not worth ruining your life for a 15-minute high." (ll. 39–40) Do you agree with Megan? Comment on her statement in about 200–250 words.

SOME COMMON MISTAKES

Hier findest du eine Übersicht mit Fehlern, die besonders häufig vorkommen.

Beispiel	***falsch***	***richtig***	***Hinweise***
(älter) als (beim Vergleich)	~~older **as**~~	older **than**	zum Ausdruck von Ungleichheit wird die Steigerungsform mit **than** verwendet
a/an	~~**an** uniform~~	**a** uniform	die Verwendung des unbestimmten Artikels hängt von der Aussprache, nicht von der Schreibung des folgendes Wortes ab
Bedingungssätze	~~If he **would come**, we would go to the cinema.~~	If he came, we would go to the cinema.	im if-Satz wird kein **would** verwendet; im Typ II muss im Nebensatz das *past* stehen.
bekommen	~~What have you **become** for Christmas?~~	What have you **got** for Christmas?	*bekommen* wird nicht mit *become*, sondern mit *get* übersetzt
es gibt	~~**It gives** a lot of unemployed people here in Germany.~~	**There are** a lot of unemployed people here in Germany.	die englische Entsprechung für *es gibt* heißt *there is* (Singular) bzw. *there are* (Plural)
feel	~~I feel **myself** ill.~~	I feel ill.	*sich fühlen* wird mit *feel* (ohne reflexive pronouns) übersetzt
gut	~~He can read **good**.~~	He can read **well**.	Um zu sagen, dass jemand etwas gut macht, benötigt man das **Adverb** *well*. Das dazugehörige Adjektiv *good* sagt aus, wie etwas ist.
hard – hardly	~~Before his exams he worked **hardly**.~~	Before his exams he worked **hard**.	Es gibt zwei Adverbien mit unterschiedlicher Bedeutung zum Adjektiv *hard (schwer, fleißig)*: *hard (schwer, fleißig)* und *hardly (kaum)*
Hausaufgaben machen	~~When do you **make** your homework?~~	When do you **do** your homework?	*Hausaufgaben machen* wird ins Englische mit *do homework* übersetzt
lassen	~~My mum **let** me work in the garden the whole afternoon.~~	My mum **made** me work in the garden the whole afternoon.	Wenn ausgedrückt werden soll, was jemand einem anderen **erlaubt**, so verwendet man **let**. Um auszudrücken, dass jemand einen anderen etwas machen lässt (im Sinne von *zwingen*), musst du *make* verwenden.
most – die meisten	~~**The** most pupils don't like doing homework.~~	**Most** pupils don't like doing homework.	die deutsche Entsprechung für *die meisten* ist *most* (ohne Artikel!)

mustn't	~~You **mustn't** help me, I can do that without you.~~	You **needn't** help me, I can do that without you.	*mustn't* bedeutet *nicht dürfen*; *nicht brauchen* bzw. *nicht müssen* wird mit *needn't* übersetzt
Relativpronomen	~~He has got an uncle **which** is a famous footballer.~~	He has got an uncle **who** is a famous footballer.	für Personen verwendet man das Relativpronomen *who*; *which* benutzt man für Dinge und Gegenstände
sensible – sensitive	~~Don't shout at her, she is very **sensible**.~~	Don't shout at her, she is very **sensitive**.	die englische Entsprechung für *sensibel* ist nicht *sensible* (was *vernünftig* heißt), sondern *sensitive*
since	~~We **wait** for him **since** 6 pm.~~	We **have been waiting** for him since 6 pm.	*since* – genau wie *for* – wird mit *seit* übersetzt und muss mit dem *present perfect* verwendet werden
viel – viele / much – many	~~How **many** time and how **much** euros have you got?~~	How **much** time and how **many** euros have you got?	Für **zählbare** Substantive verwendet man *many*, für **nicht zählbare** Substantive *much*. Beachte auch, dass man **much** und **many** hauptsächlich **in Fragen und verneinten Sätzen verwendet**; in bejahten Sätzen benutzt man meist *a lot of/lots of*.
von (beim Passiv)	~~The book was written **from** J. K. Rowling.~~	The book was written **by** J. K. Rowling.	um auszudrücken, *von wem* etwas gemacht wird, verwendet man *by*
vor (zeitlich)	~~**For** six years she started playing the guitar.~~	Six years **ago** she started playing the guitar.	die deutsche Entsprechung für *vor* (einer bestimmten Zeit) ist nicht *for*, sondern *ago*
want	~~I want **that you come** with me.~~	I want **you to come** with me.	an Stelle von *that* verwendet man nach *want* ein *Objekt + to + Infinitiv* um auszudrücken, dass man will, dass andere etwas tun
wollen	~~What **will** you do now?~~	What do you **want to** do now?	*wollen* wird nicht mit *will*, sondern mit *want* übersetzt
Wortstellung	~~He can **fast** run.~~	He can run **fast**.	Adverbien der Art und Weise wie *fast* stehen nicht zwischen Hilfs- und Vollverb, sondern nach dem (Voll)Verb bzw. dessen Objekt.

Lösungen zu Seite 8

1. Conditional sentences
   a) If Bink's brother hadn't been going through a difficult time, Bink wouldn't have run away./wouldn't have wanted some attention.
   b) If Bink hadn't seen a placard advertising her disappearance, she wouldn't have written a message to her family and gone to school.
   c) If her violin teacher hadn't seen the placard after having talked to her, she wouldn't have phoned the police.
   d) If the police hadn't found her, Bink wouldn't have returned home.
2. Reported Speech
   Bink said that she still didn't know why she had run away. Her mum believed that it had been because her brother had been going through a difficult time and she had wanted some attention. Maybe that was true, but if so, it had been entirely subconscious.

Lösungen zu Seite 9

3. Questions
   Why did you run away?
   Where did you go after leaving your house?
   Where did you spend the night?
   What did you feel when you saw the placard advertising your disappearance?
   Who phoned the police?
   What was it like when you returned home?
4. Writing
   a) summary of Bink's story
   Bink, now 15, runs away from home at the age of 12, not being aware of her brother being probably the reason. After having spent two days and a night on the streets, she gets to know that she has been reported missing and they look for her and she decides to contact her parents. A teacher she meets by accident phones the police who find Bink and take her home. It takes some time until she realizes what she has done to her family. *(85 words)*
   b) Stuarts Future
   Stuart spends a year in a state of insecurity, searching and resignation. After he leaves school, he tries to find a job. He is fired from a call centre where he works because he is rude to customers. Then he washes cars and sells rubber dinosaurs in coffeeshops. He continues to have a bad relationship with his mother who changes partners frequently and has a drinking problem. Luckily, Stuart hates and avoids alcohol because he's a sportsman. Stuart has been playing hockey since he was five years old. He is a very good player and has some friends and mentors at the club. At the age of 17, he is offered a contract to play on the first hockey team of Arsenal London and is finally able to rent a flat of his own. *(134 words)*
   c) comment writing
   Society should offer help to runaways if their parents are not able or willing to bring up their children.
   It's my intention to discuss if society should help runaways if their parents can't or don't want to do this. Although I firmly believe in family life, I must admit that there are cases in which it is better for both parents and especially their children when they are taken care of by society. So I agree with the given statement.
   It goes without saying that the best way for a child to grow up is in an intact family. But with a high divorce rate like in Germany, plenty of kids grow up in single-parent households today. Moreover, for some of these single parents it is too much to handle a job, the household and a kid or even two.
   Unfortunately, also the unemployment rate is constantly rising and thus a growing number of single mothers (and fathers) have to rely on social welfare. Sometimes it's not far away from poverty to alcohol or drug abuse, leading to neglecting children or even abusing them. If children of such families decide to leave their homes, it's society's task to care for them. Although a state-run institution can never replace a real family, at least it can offer some youths chances they wouldn't have if staying in their broken families or/and to protect them against violence and abuse.
   So I've come to the conclusion that if parents are really not able or willing to raise their children, it might be better if these children get help offered by the state. *(248 words)*

Lösungen zu Seite 13

2. *Possible Answers:*
   Text A a) The risks they face are being vulnerable to sexual and physical abuse, potential stealing or begging and sleeping on the streets.
   b) Being a victim of bullying, not doing well in school subjects, feeling excluded, skipping classes and being afraid of their parents' reaction could lead young people to run away from home.
   Text B a) "Winterwatch" was launched to provide emergency accommodation for people suffering due to the cold weather.

b) Most of the homes they live in are cold, old, run down, perhaps mouldy and damp.

3. a/1, b/3, c/11, d/12, e/6, f/8, g/9, h/5, i/2, j/4, k/7, l/10
4. *Remember it is important to write how YOU feel. The task calls for PERSONAL RESPONSE: Your ideas supported by examples from the text may be positive or negative depending on how you respond to the appeal. Your answer should include the following points:*
   - *an opening statement which states in general the impression the appeal makes on you*
     e.g. It touches me emotionally and makes me aware of the suffering some people endure in cold weather.
     It makes me sensitive to other people's suffering.
     It makes me feel sad and forces me to realize/think about the suffering of other people. I feel prompted to help.
   - *comment(s) regarding the title e.g.* The title is very effective. The word "shelter" immediately suggests a refuge and "campaign for the homeless" ascertains at a glance what the appeal is all about.
     The title grabs the reader's attention and lures him into reading the appeal.
     The title is not very effective because it is too obvious.
   - *comments on language e.g.* The language used in the appeal is informative but heavily emotive and persuasive. The writer wishes to persuade readers, to tell them how they should act. In this case – donate to their appeal. He or she also intends to move our hearts so that we do the "morally right thing".
     I think the language used is manipulative because the writer tries to coerce readers into "buying" his idea.
   - *comment(s) on tone e.g.* The tone of the appeal is persuasive and emotional. The writer appeals to his/her readers for help. The language used in the appeal contributes to this general feeling.
   - *comment(s) on layout e.g.* The layout of the appeal reminds us of an advertisement and it certainly functions similarly. Key words are in bold letters and the example in italics is for emphasis. The writer's aim is to sell his product or idea as is the case with ads.
   - *comment(s) on examples e.g.* The examples reinforce the writer's intention to convince readers to help his cause. Again here, the example encourages us to feel sympathy for the victim, Shelley, and relief that she had been given aid before it was too late.

Lösungen zu Seite 14

5. *Model answer:*
   Your writing will involve the elements of a speech since you will be addressing your audience personally. It is necessary to maintain your audience's interest for the entire 3 minutes. Careful choice of language and examples can help you achieve this.
   - *Address your audience:* Good morning, parents, teachers and fellow students.
   - *catchy example:*
     Did you know approximately 5,000 teenagers under 16 run away each year. (We do not have statistics for Germany, but we can assume that they are similar to Scotland's) and / or:
     15 year old Linda ran away from home. It took two weeks to find her. She was an emotional wreck; she had been sleeping rough, beaten up by rowdies and begging on the streets. Why did this happen? Linda had been teased and bullied by her classmates because she wasn't cool enough, put down by her parents for being a social failure and ignored by the boy she idolised. She felt lonely, lost and trapped.
   - *Who are we, what do we want, why, how can you help?*
     We at Runaway Refuge believe this should not happen. We want teenagers to know there is help out there if they need it. Our emergency homes provide a shelter and give teenagers a chance to try and solve their problems before taking drastic steps. We have professionals on hand, volunteer social workers and counsellors who will listen and offer constructive assistance. But to provide these services ladies and gentlemen, we need your financial support. Please donate to Runaway Refuge and help prevent someone you love from ending up on the streets.

Lösungen zu Seite 16

1. a) The Opera
   b) Manhattan
   c) the Sydney Tower
   d) Doyle's or Kables
   e) it used to be a former governor's wife's lookout

Lösungen zu Seite 17

2. a) ... there are people from many different ethnic backgrounds living there.
   b) ... protect swimmers from shark attacks / to prevent sharks from entering the swimming areas.
   c) ... you can always buy restricted view tickets or try getting last minute, half-price ones at Halftix.
   d) ... should visit the Art Gallery in Sydney.
   e) ... be seen at Balls Head Reserve.

Lösungen zu Seite 18

2. a) She has to join the team in secret because her traditional Indian parents do not approve of girls playing soccer.
   b) They would both like to be professional soccer players.
   c) I think it's because Jules' mother feels her tomboy daughter who has no interest in girlish activities as well as a close friendship with another soccer loving girl could be nothing but a lesbian.

Lösungen zu Seite 19

3. a) coming of age, b) facing, c) touching, d) blown her whistle, e) forgive, f) unlike
4. The director deserves as many awards as she can fit on her mantelpiece. Bend it like Beckham is a must-see, a real feel good film of wonderful characters. It is colourful, exciting and absolutely hilarious.
5.

Playing soccer	Reasons For	Against
	– like sport – am a good soccer player – made the team – it's my life – am old enough to make my own decisions – don't live in India, but in London – parents should learn to be more tolerant	– parents disapprove – don't want to hurt them – should be proud of my Indian traditions and obey my parents – after all soccer will come and go, but family will always be there

Lösungen zu Seite 20

2. a) I would read the poem in a frustrated and angry tone of voice.
   b) The poet has created a very realistic situation for the readers. Since he has written the poem from the point of view of the student, he uses words that are common for a "fed up" sixth former who has had enough of his family's nagging.
   c) The poem is written in rhyming couplets. The pattern is aa, bb, cc, dd etc. I believe the poet has chosen this pattern because it makes the poem sound like a chant – easy to memorize and repetitive. What the sixth former hears all the time from his dad, mum and gran is always the same; it is monotonous and repetitive.

Lösungen zu Seite 21

3. a) He's probably about 16 or 17 years old (sixth form). Yes, most youths of that age often feel as if there are worlds of difference between their parents and themselves (the generation gap). They feel misjudged, misunderstood, ignored and generally pressured into doing what their parents think is best.
   b)

Boy	Father	Mother	Grandmother
– just wants to be left alone – father should disappear – mother should move out – wants to go out and have a good time – doesn't want to have arguments with his parents all the time. – Gran should go away and leave him alone and /or keep her mouth shut – probably doesn't want to be a clerk	– probably would like his son to dress differently (more conservatively) – wishes to have a "perfect son" (a high achiever, respectful etc.)	– wants her son to do well in school so that he can get a decent job in an office	– wants the boy to speak more politely and be as gallant as the boys of her youth

4. a) *Suggested Answers:*
   – doesn't appear to have high self-esteem
   – parents constantly nagging him to be different, do not accept him as he is
   – feels isolated in family, like a misfit
   – going out is a means of escape
   – seems to want to forget problems rather than face them
   b) Hi Sam,
   How's it going? Right now life at home is sheer hell for me. Man, my father is constantly on my back ...
   He's such a pain, always going on about how I dress like a bum and look like one too. He'd like me to say, "yes sir" and "no sir" and be some perfect little nerd. Why can't he just accept that the fashions are different from when he was my age. What a loser! And then there's my old lady. Can you believe she'd like me to be a clerk. I'd rather die than work in some boring old office. She keeps harassing me to study more to make sure I finish 6th form.
   I hope you have an easier time at home. At least your gran doesn't live with you. Mine can't stop talking about

the good old days and how young people today show no respect for their elders and how I'm so uncouth. I tell you Sam, I can't wait to get out of here. Then at least I don't have to listen to my folks' broken record all the time. I have to make sure I finish 6th form and get a job – anything to escape.
There's a hip hop band playing at the Midnight Club Saturday night. Wanna go?
Take it easy.

Cheers,
Tim

Lösungen zu Seite 22

1. *Suggested Answers:*
   a) Since she has money, she probably bribed him or blackmailed him. She may have also roughed him up a bit given that her hair was all tousled.
   b) Barry Kent is a bully at Adrian's school. He is ill-mannered / rough (called Adrian bad names) and aggressive (hung Adrian to a coat hook and duffed him up).
   c) He probably doesn't since no one came to his rescue in the cloakroom. He also makes reference to his lonely life as an intellectual.
   d) Adrian uses colloquial / informal spoken language in his diary.
   e) Adrian thinks she is not very smart and not a model mother.
2. *Model Answer:*

   Friday, May 22nd
   Couldn't believe it, Barry Kent was actually nice to me at school today. Gran must've given him a real fright. He didn't even try to blackmail me. What a relief that I didn't have to turn over all my allowance money to him. I must write a poem today. Intellectuals like me need to spend time doing that kind of stuff. My father's being a right pain – wish he could get a job then he'd stay out of my way. He and my mother have been yelling at each other again. On TV the parents are always kissing and speaking softly to each other – not in our house though. Figured; I'd be stuck with this lot.

Lösungen zu Seite 24

2. ▪ An extraordinary achievement' (Sunday Times)
   ▪ 'A terrifically entertaining and imaginative story wrapped round its tough, thoughtprovoking philosophical heart' (Independent on Sunday)
   ▪ 'Sophie's World is set to become a unique popular classic: a wonderfully engaging mystery story that also form a completely accessible and lucid introduction to philosophy and philosophers' (The Times)
3. ▪ collect old coins or foreign stamps
   ▪ do needle work
   ▪ spend time on a particular sport
   ▪ enjoy reading / reading tastes differ, newspaper, comics, novels, books on astronomy, wildlife, technological discoveries
   ▪ be interested in horses or stones
   ▪ watch all the sports programs on TV
4. Basic needs: food; warmth, love, care; company of others
   Philosophical interests / questions:
   – What is the most important thing in life?
   – Why are we here?
   – Who are we?
   But when these basic needs have been satisfied – will there still be something that everybody needs?
5. An excerpt from a novel, a letter to Sophie, the main character.
6. The debate is as old as mankind itself.
7. *Possible Answers:*
   a) the answer is a new job.
   b) the answer is getting pregnant.
   c) the answer is to find some consolation and to be able to sleep at night.
   d) the answer is safety for his money.
   e) the answer is to make the world safe for democracy.
   f) the answer is a new organ.
   g) the answer is more patience.

Lösungen zu Seite 26

1. a) 'To wit', said the owl.
   b) 'How many claws am I holding up?' the secretary bird said.
   c) 'He's God', cried all the other creatures again.
   d) 'He's God', screamed a Plymouth Rock hen.
   e) 'Aren't you afraid?' the secretary bird asked.
   f) 'Can he see in the daytime, too?' asked a red fox.
2. The secretary bird hastened back to the other creatures and reported, "The owl is indeed the greatest and wisest animal in the world because he can see in the dark and because he can answer any question."
   The other creatures sent a messenger to the owl and he asked, "Would you be our leader?"
3. Once upon a starless midnight there was an owl who sat on the branch of an oak tree. Two ground moles tried to slip quietly by, unnoticed. 'You!' said the owl. 'Who?' they quavered, in fear and astonishment, for they could not believe it was possible for anyone to see them in that thick darkness. 'You two!' said the owl. The moles hurried away and told the other creatures of the field and forest that the owl was the greatest and wisest of all animals because he could see in the dark and because he could answer any question. 'I'll see about that', said a secretary bird, and he called on the owl one night when it was again very dark. 'How many claws am I holding up?' said the secretary bird, 'Two', said the owl, and that was right. 'Can you give me another expression for "that is to say" or "namely"?' asked the secretary bird. 'To wit', said the owl. 'Why does a lover call on his love?' asked the secretary bird. 'Tu woo', said the owl.
   The secretary bird hastened back to the other creatures and reported that the owl was indeed the greatest and wisest animal in the world because he could see in the dark and because he could answer any question. 'Can he see in the day-time, too?' asked a red fox. 'Yes', echoed a dormouse and a French poodle. 'Can he see in the day-time, too?' All the other creatures laughed loudly at this silly question, and they set upon the red fox and his friends and drove them out of the region. Then they sent a messenger to the owl and asked him to be their leader. When the owl appeared among the animals it was high noon and the sun was shining brightly. He walked very slowly, which gave him an appearance of great dignity, and he peered about him with large, staring eyes, which gave him an air of tremendous importance. 'He's God!' screamed a Plymouth Rock hen. And the others took up the cry 'He's God!' So they followed him wherever he went and when he began to bump into things they begun to bump into things, too. Finally he came to a concrete highway and he started up the middle of it and all the other creatures followed him. Presently a hawk, who was acting as outrider, observed a truck coming toward them at fifty miles an hour, and he reported to the secretary bird and the secretary bird reported to the owl. 'There's danger ahead', said the secretary bird. 'To wit'? said the owl. The secretary bird told him. 'Aren't you afraid?' he asked. 'Who?' said the owl calmly, for he could not see the truck. 'He's God!' cried all the creatures again, and they were still crying 'He's God!' when the truck hit them and ran them down. Some of the animals were merely injured, but most of them, including the owl, were killed.
   Moral: You can fool too many of people too much of the time.

Lösungen zu Seite 27

4. Example: The owl could have a deep and serious voice.
   The moles … soft …; The red fox … clever / tricky …
   The secretary bird … loud / convincing / doubtful …
   A French poodle / the dormouse … faithful / quiet …
   The Plymouth Rock hen … faithful / inspired / delighted …
   A hawk … serious / helpful / doubtful …
   All the creatures … impressive / enthusiastic …
5. a) The owl can see them in the dark. The owl can answer "any" question.
   b) He asked him some questions to find out whether the owl was as clever as the moles maintained.
   c) The owl could convince the secretary bird by answering the two questions.
   d) He asked whether the owl could see in the daytime, too?
   e) The way he walked impressed the animals. His large staring eyes made him look very important and he seemed omnipotent in face of danger.
   f) The animals followed the owl to the highway disregarding the truck which was drawing nearer.
   g) The owl kept calm because he could not see the truck.
   h) All of them are male. "He" is used in the text. The mouse can be male or female. There is no direct hint in the text.
   i) The truck hit and killed most of the animals including the owl.
6. *siehe Text*

Lösungen zu Seite 28

7. They could have bellowed, "Go away and never come back."
   A mouse could have screamed, "You're a liar. Shut up"
   The creatures could have roared, "You're not here. If you can't trust him, go away."
   "Bloody liar", they could have hollered.
   A dormouse could have raised her voice, "We don't tolerate such an idea".
8. *Possible Answers:*
   In general blind obedience has two sides. On the one hand it is very important in private life. On the other hand everyone must reflect on relationships in their private and professional life. You cannot trust just anybody, especially strangers. As far as the media is concerned you must be critical of information.
9. *Possible Answers:*
   persons you obey blindly can be: your mother, your father, your brothers and sisters, your friends, your teachers at primary school, doctors, members of the same peer group, people of the same religion / belief, politicians
   the reasons for blind obedience can be: love, friendship, understanding, the structure of relationships, similar interests, dependence, natural authorities

Lösungen zu Seite 30

2. 1. – f), 2. – h), 3. – q), 4. – c), 5. – j), 6. – k), 7. – g), 8. – m), 9. – d), 10. – a), 11. – n), 12. – l), 13. – e), 14 – i), 15. – b), 16. – o), 17. – p).
3. *Possible Answer:*
   Husband: Are you mad? How could you call my boss after midnight?
   Wife: Honey, I did it for you, too. I couldn't remain silent. It was such a dangerous and an embarrassing situation. Imagine your boss had been poisoned and didn't know anything about the cat and the salmon.
   Husband: We should have waited longer.
   Wife: How was I to know the real story?
   Husband: You are usually quite good at looking into the future.
   Wife: Really? It seems to me you are looking for a person you can blame for the evening.
   Husband: That's totally unfair. The party was absolutely important for my career. I can't imagine going to the office again. How should I behave and react? I don't know what to do.
   Woman: Come on, don't be so afraid. Work and behave as usual. After all, the evening wasn't a complete disaster!

Lösungen zu Seite 31

4. *Possible Answer:*
   Next day in the company
   The young man takes his wife's advice and does not say anything about the previous night. His boss ignores the late night phone call and says thank you for the wonderful evening and the delicious meal.
5. Z. 4: after cleaning it; Z. 5: Returning; Z. 5/6: sitting; Z. 6: chewing; Z. 10: making; Z. 11: Closing; Z. 13: Racking; Z. 14: Thinking; Z. 15: including; Z. 20: looking.
6. *Possible Answer:*
   B: I'm afraid Mr. Taylor is not available / is not in.
   A: Oh, I see. Have you got any idea when he'll be in / he'll be available?
   B: No, I don't know. Can I give him a message? ...
   A: No, I'm afraid not. I must speak to him now.
   B: Could he call you back?
   A: Oh, sorry but I have to warn Mr Taylor. You see he was a guest at our dinner party and something rather unfortunate happened – our poor cat died last night. I fear the fish it ate was contaminated. Our cat got the same salmon I used for the salmon mousse. I'm so sorry. But I think Mr. Taylor should contact a doctor ...
7. *siehe Text*

Lösungen zu Seite 33

1. a) He means that rap functions in the same way as a legitimate country. It is a microcosm with its leaders (politicians – the musicians) and followers (listeners – civilians) politics, and decision-making processes.
   b) They patrol the hiphop nation because there is a need for protection and control when negative events such as group wars and internal conflicts take place.
   c) Rap music can influence racial and social discrimination and worsen it. Rap music can also cause individuals to feel justified in their prejudiced notions and breed increasing hatred.
   d) Hiphop needs to revolutionise itself; it should be a way of bringing people together and influencing positive change rather than leading to more violence and negativity.
2. 1-a, 2-b, 3-c, 4-a, 5-c, 6-a, 7-b, 8-b, 9-c, 10-a

3. a) false, b) false, c) true, d) true, e) false, f) true, g) false, h) false
4. *Model Answer:*
   Yes: Given the enormous influence popular culture has on today's youth, I think it is important that the music young people listen to provides them with positive messages. Lyrics to popular songs are easy to memorize and listeners find themselves repeating these automatically. The messages conveyed in lyrics are therefore registered subliminally. If these are negative they could contribute to negative behaviour.
   Teenagers are impressionable and often victims of peer pressure. The desire to belong and be accepted often pushes them to act inappropriately. Popular music is an integral part of youth culture –The artist and the music provide young people with something they can identify with. Therefore if the ideas in this music are violent or negative, they could lead to more violence, sexual promiscuity, drug use etc. among today's youth. It takes a strong individual to say no, to think critically and to maintain a sense of self in a world full of temptations.

Lösungen zu Seite 34

1. To peter.mueller@btx.net
   From frank.werner@hotsnail.com
   Date 25 June 2006
   Subject Invitation

   Hi Peter

   It's my birthday on 2 July. It would be great if you could come to my party at my house at 8 pm. Don't forget to bring a big present ;-)

   Frank

Lösungen zu Seite 35

1. Dear Granny, 24 August 2006

   I'm writing to you to say thank you for the birthday present I got from you. You've been so generous! I'm really happy because now Miriam and I can plan our trip to England. In my last letter I told you about our dream – my best friend's and mine – to see London. I've seen and heard so much about it but I've never been there. We're looking forward to visiting all those great sights – the Tower, the London Dungeon, Madame Tussaud's and many more. I'm taking Dad's new digital camera with me and I'll send you some of my best photos, I promise.
   How are you? What about your leg? Does it still hurt? I hope you can walk without pain now.
   Mum says she wants to phone you next weekend. Then we'll be able to talk to each other.

   Take care
   Anne

Lösungen zu Seite 37

1. *individuelle Lösung*
2. *individuelle Lösung*

Lösungen zu Seite 40

1. The story *"The fun they had"* is set in the USA in the year 2157. It is about Margie (11), and Tommy (13) who has found a book about school in the past, which means school in our time. Their world differs a lot from ours. The children are really surprised to find a book because books do not exist any longer in the year 2157. Everything they usually read is on the screen of a computer.
   When Margie gets to know what the book is about, she does not know what one could write about school, because she hates it. Contrary to us, children in the future do not go to school any more, but have a computer as their teacher at home. Tommy tells Margie about schools in the past when children went to school and learned together with a human teacher – an idea Margie likes a lot. *(151 words)*

Lösungen zu Seite 41

2. Dear diary, May 17, 2157

   Today Tommy found a real book!
   I've never seen such a thing before! It's totally crazy. The words on this printed paper stand still and you turn these yellow and crinkly pages and when you turn back to the page before, there are still the same words on it that it

had when you read it for the first time. What a waste! But it is so fascinating. Tommy said he had found it in the attic. Unfortunately we don't have one. Perhaps I should ask granddad because he once told me that his granddad had told him that there had been a time when all stories had been written on paper.
And when Tommy showed me his book (he was a little posey about it) he told me about school in the past because that's what the book is about. Imagine – they didn't have a regular teacher but a man. I can't believe that a man is smart enough to be a teacher, but the kids didn't have to spend a lot of boring time in front of their teachers, no, they went to a special building where they met their teacher! What a wonderful thing to be together with all these kids the whole morning. What a lot of fun they must have had!

Yours,
Margie
(220 words)

Lösungen zu Seite 44

1. *Possible Answer:*
The story of "The Meeting" is set in Johannesburg, South Africa during the time of Apartheid. It is about two 17-year-old girls who happen to meet each other near a park one day. Candy, who is white, twists her ankle and is offered help by Becky, a pretty black girl. While talking they get to know each other a little, and Candy realizes that she likes her despite her initial mistrust caused by her upbringing. Before Candy phones her father to fetch her, the girls agree to meet again. When Candy's father arrives, he shows no interest in Becky although his daughter praises her so much. Finally he realizes that Candy wants him to thank her as well but, misunderstanding the whole situation, offers her a tip, which Becky refuses and considers an insult. *(134 words)*

Lösungen zu Seite 45

2. *Possible Answer:*
Becky suddenly turned and walked off. Meanwhile Candy's father got impatient. "Why doesn't she want to take the money? Isn't it enough?!" he asked his daughter. Instead of answering his question, Candy shouted, "Becky, please wait!" To her father's surprise, Becky was running away.
"Let's get into the car," he said. While driving home, Candy tried to explain to her father what had happened. But he didn't really understand. So Candy didn't tell him about their intention to meet again since she was afraid he wouldn't allow her to see Becky again anyway. In the evening, when Candy was lying in bed, she thought about what to tell Becky next Wednesday when they would meet again. She was wondering how she could explain her dad's behaviour to her and say sorry. Hopefully Becky would come as Candy wished so much. There were so many things she wanted to talk about with her ... *(153 words)*

3. *Possible Answer:*

Candy and her father drove off. On their way home Candy said nothing for a while.

Dad: Why are you so quiet? What's wrong with you? Does your foot still hurt?
Candy: No, it's not because of my foot. It's ... you know ... I mean ... How could you be so rude to Becky?
D: You call me rude? What are you talking about? She is just a black girl. Should I have invited her to dinner tonight?
C: Please, be serious.
D: I am serious. She helped you and that's nice, I understand, but don't you think she was rude when she refused the money I offered to her? Is she too proud to accept a tip from a white man? It's obvious she's poor. She was wearing such terrible, ragged clothes! By the way, have you still got your purse? I wouldn't be surprised to find out that she ran away with it!
C: But Dad, that's exactly what I thought at the beginning, too. But you are being unfair. It's the same old story you've been telling me my whole life. Blacks are inferior, dirty, dishonest, uneducated ...
D: And it's true!
C: No Dad, it isn't. Becky is wonderful. She is pretty and has a good sense of humour. She made me laugh several times although I was in pain. And of course she is honest. She didn't rob me. And by the way, do you know why she didn't take your money? She didn't want it because you don't pay a friend for helping you.
D: A friend?
C: Yes, we've become friends and I'm looking forward to seeing her again.
D: You won't see her again. A black girl and a white girl can't be friends, not in our society. Don't forget this! So, here we are at the doctor's. I want Mr Deep to check your foot. And please no talking about that black girl any longer.

Candy decided not to tell her dad about their agreement to meet each other again ... *(332 words)*

Lösungen zu Seite 46

1. *Possible Answer:*
   Throughout the history of mankind people have oppressed each other. The white man conquered the native people of America and Australia, as well as the blacks he had taken from Africa as slaves, to name just a couple of examples.
   So are some people more equal than others or are all people equal, no matter who they are or where they are from? In my opinion there can only be one answer to this question: As we are all human beings, it goes without saying that we are all equal. On the other hand, reality shows that racial prejudice still exists and inequality can be found worldwide.
   Nearly 150 years ago, Abraham Lincoln put an end to slavery with the Emancipation Declaration of 1863, which was only put into practice after the end of the Civil War two years later. Then a time of segregation followed which lasted as long as the Civil Rights Movement when Martin Luther King fought for equal rights for black people. Finally, black people as well as Native Americans were granted full rights. But does this really mean that they were then or are really equal to whites today? According to the law, they are, but more subtle forms of racial discrimination have replaced the obvious ones. Of course, we all know famous and successful Afro-Americans – just think of actors, singers and sportsmen. But what about the high unemployment rate among blacks or the high proportion of black people on death row? Moreover, there are parallels to this development when we look at South Africa after the time of Apartheid or at what is happening to Aborigines in Australia.
   In addition, globalisation causes the widening of the gap between the rich and the poor. Still and perhaps more than ever the developed countries benefit from the so called developing countries, thus leading to more political, economic and social inequalities.
   With the attack on September 11, 2001 and Bush's war on terrorism, tensions between Muslims and the western world have grown making it difficult to establish equality or simply a better understanding and tolerance of people of different origins and religious backgrounds.
   All in all, there is no denying that we are all (biologically speaking) equal and no people have the right to say they are superior to other nations. But there are so many examples in history and at present which show that a lot of people including leading politicians do not accept this notion. This leads me to the conclusion that these inequalities will continue to exist in the near future. *(433 words)*

Lösungen zu Seite 49

1. a) *Possible answers:*
   The picture I want to describe is an oil painting which shows part of a room with an open French window. In the background of the picture there is the corner of a room with the French window to the right. Because of a light breeze, the curtain is moving. There is also a mirror on the right hand-side. I can see two chairs standing in front of the mirror as well as two wall lamps and the mirror images of a part of a painting hanging on the wall and a piece of furniture. The left hand side of the corner looks nearly empty apart from a carpet or runner and a piece of furniture. There is nothing on that wall except some grey or white colour. It looks as if someone has painted the wall carelessly to cover something that has been there before. There is no person to be seen either. The only signs of life or movement is caused by the curtain moving in the wind, which gets into the room because of the open window and the rays of sunlight on the floor, which can be seen in the foreground. These together with the dominantly brown colours also give the (otherwise) deserted room a warm and pleasant expression. As the room doesn't give the impression that it is inhabited, it might be a room in a castle, palace or museum. This idea is reinforced by the decorated ceiling, which you mainly find in older buildings and the fact that the whole room seems to be furnished in an antique style, too. *(267 words)*

   b) I like the picture because I think it shows the room of an old castle, which I love visiting. They are so different from the houses we live in today and therefore really interesting. In my mind it is fascinating to speculate on people who might have lived there and things that might have happened there. When I look at the picture, lots of associations come into my mind. Why does the painted wall in the background look the way it does or who has opened the window and why? I'd like to be there, looking at the room and the other rooms nearby and after stepping out of the room, walk through the French window to enjoy the warm sunlight and the breeze outside.
   (128 words)

   c) Susan: Look at this oil painting. Isn't it beautiful?
   Kevin: Beautiful? I don't know. Quite ordinary and boring, I think.
   Susan: Ordinary? Boring? You're kidding?
   Kevin: No, I'm serious. What makes you think it is beautiful?
   Susan: Well, I like the atmosphere created by the warm colours and antique furniture always fascinates me.
   Kevin: Old boring stuff. No people, no action, no atmosphere. No, this painting doesn't appeal to me at all because it doesn't tell me anything. There isn't even much to see. I'm asking myself why the painter didn't find anything more interesting to paint rather than such an ugly wall and why are the chairs standing like this in

the room and not the other way around so that two people can see each other when they sit there and want to talk? I would have painted something in the background instead of the grey wall. No, I don't understand at all what you like about this painting.
Susan: Oh, it's probably exactly what you dislike about it. It makes me think why the things are arranged in that order. I mean, for example the wall in the background. I can imagine that there used to stand a wardrobe or cupboard and the woman who owns it didn't like it any longer so they sold it or gave it away. The room is in their cottage where they – she and her family – only live in the warm season. So they removed the old piece of furniture last autumn and they have just returned to their cottage to stay there for the summer. Therefore they have opened the French window to let some fresh air into the room. Next week the new wardrobe will be delivered.
Kevin: Oh, Susan, please stop. We are looking at a terrible picture and you're telling me a whole story about something which isn't there. Let us please move on and look at some nicer pictures.
Susan: Okay, I just wanted to explain to you why I think this is a great painting.
Kevin: Thank you, I hope you don't mind me walking on.
Susan: Oh, please wait, I'm coming with you... *(363 words)*

2. a) The picture I want to describe is quite a modern painting which looks nearly as realistic as a photo. In the foreground you see a night-bar or coffee bar which is filled with just four people including the bartender who you can see on the right hand-side. The three guests are a man sitting with his back to the viewer and a couple looking at and probably talking to the bartender. The bar is illuminated in a very bright and cold light, supporting the uninviting and sterile atmosphere of the bar and the whole picture. You can see lots of empty bar stools but there is no sign of any people who might enter the bar, which is called "Phillies" and the walls are to a great extent made of glass so that we can look inside. There are no pictures or any other kind of decoration to be seen. In the background and on the left hand-side you can see a house covered in darkness as you can only recognize two shop windows and the Venetian blinds of some flats on the first floor. The empty street and pavement lit by the bar's light can be seen in the foreground. The whole picture evokes a feeling of loneliness and abandonment, in my view. It seems as if this scene is set in a city late at night and the guests don't want to go home because there is no one waiting for them. All in all it is rather sad and hopeless. *(253 words)*

   b) I wouldn't like to be one of the people in the picture because they don't look very happy. Although I'm not old enough to sit in a bar at night, I would only like to be there with my friends enjoying myself. Without friends it isn't nice at all. On the other hand, I hope that I will have a family later who is waiting for me in the evening to come home so that there will be no reason for me to go to a bar alone at night. The bar and the surroundings don't look that inviting either. I prefer places where plenty of people meet and not such a lonely bar. Such a bar with few guests is probably boring for the bartender who has too few persons to talk to or serve. The male guest doesn't seem to have anyone to talk to and I think the couple isn't that happy either, otherwise they wouldn't sit in such a miserable bar.
   All in all I'm glad I'm not any of these people nor in such a situation. *(177 words)*

Lösungen zu Seite 53

2. *Possible Answers:*
Vorüberlegungen:
Gemma hat die Nacht mit ihrem Freund Tar verbracht, ohne, wie ursprünglich geplant, mit ihm zu schlafen. Da Tar von zu Hause wegläuft, wird sie ihn vielleicht nie wieder oder zumindest eine lange Zeit nicht sehen. Sie hatte aber gespürt, dass er gerade jetzt ihre Gesellschaft braucht, da er keinerlei Liebe in seinem Elternhaus bekommt. Sein Vater ist Alkoholiker und hat ihn wiederholt geschlagen. Als Gemma nach Hause kommt, sind ihre Eltern sehr verärgert und machen ihr Vorwürfe, da sie ihr nicht trauen. Bereits im ersten Abschnitt des Textes wird klar, dass das Verhältnis schon längere Zeit sehr angespannt sein muss, sonst hätte Gemma nicht so eine negative Meinung von ihren Eltern. Während ihre Mutter recht zurückhaltend reagiert und versucht, zu vermitteln, rastet ihr Vater immer mehr aus und nennt sie eine Lügnerin. Dies muss sehr verletzend auf Gemma wirken, die ihre Eltern in diesem Falle nicht belogen hat. Ihre Eltern orientieren sich an alten Klischees, anstatt mit ihrer Tochter zu kommunizieren. Gemma befindet sich nunmehr in einer schwierigen emotionalen Lage, die sie sicherlich zum Thema des heutigen Tagebucheintrags machen würde. Nahe liegend ist, dass sie über die Nacht mit Tar schreibt, über den durch seinen Fortgang bedingten Verlust und auch über die für sie als sehr ungerecht empfundene Auseinandersetzung mit ihren Eltern, insbesondere mit ihrem Vater.
Wichtig ist hier auch die richtige Stilebene zu treffen. Gemmas Sprache ist eher informell, umgangssprachlich und könnte in einem Tagebucheintrag oder Brief an Tar auch Slang enthalten.

   a) Dear diary, 12 June 2005

   Liar! He calls me a liar! He doesn't have a clue how he hurts me all the time. Will he ever trust me again? Why didn't I run away together with Tar? Then I would feel much better now.
   Yes, Tar has left for good. You know, he couldn't stand his father hitting the bottle and then beating him up all

the time. On the other hand, I don't know how I'll be able to cope with this – being without Tar, especially now as it's become so difficult to get along with Mum and Dad. I'm sure Mum would understand if she listened to me but Dad ...
Perhaps I wouldn't feel so bad if I had had sex with Tar. First I thought I wanted to do it just for Tar and as a nice memory. But he didn't show me that he wanted it. I think it was more important for him that I was there with him, close to him, touching him. Suddenly all this sex stuff wasn't important to me any longer. I think it was OK. But I miss him so much.
Now I have only you.

Yours,
Gemma *(202 words)*

b) *Siehe Vorüberlegungen zu 1.*

12 June 2005

Dear Tar,

I'm so glad you gave me your friend's address so that I can let you know what life is like for me now that you've left.
How are you? Do you feel better now miles away from your brutal dad? And miles away from me? I can't understand why I let you go. When I came home the morning after our last night in the garage all hell broke loose. Dad went apeshit and mum wasn't really able to stop him. Since then we've hardly spoken. They only keep asking me where you are because they know that you haven't returned home since then and feel sorry for your lousy dad who does his best to show everyone how sorry and worried he feels! I can't stand this any longer. Please, Tar, I must leave home. I've already planned to come and see you. I'm prepared to leave everyone and everything behind me now, I really mean it. So let me know when we can talk on the phone.

Take care
Gemma
(180 words)

c) I couldn't believe my ears. Why had I talked to them and told them the truth only to have him call me liar? 'I hate you!', I said. 'There was a time when I loved you more than anyone else in the world, but now the only feeling I have is hatred.' I wanted to add 'And you will never see me again' but I bit my lip not to tell them what was going through my mind at that moment.
I left the room, slamming the door behind me. Of course, they followed me, but they were too slow. I ran into my room, locked the door, fell on my bed and cried. Mum and dad took turns trying to make me open the door and let them talk to me but I didn't. Finally I fell asleep for some hours. When I woke up, everything that had happened that day and the terrible feelings were suddenly there again. It was quiet in the house and when I looked at the alarm clock I could see that it was after midnight. I remembered what I thought of doing when dad called me liar – running away. So I opened my wardrobe, put some clothes into a bag I found under my bed and left my room and the house as quietly as I could. I had saved some money which would do until I met up with Tar. Unlike my parents, he would be happy to see me, I was sure. *(251 words)*

3. *Possible Answers:*
Being a teenager can be a hard thing, especially when it comes to the relationship with your parents. Most young people complain about their parents not allowing them the freedom and independence they need. So let me discuss if there should be rules and limits for children even if they are teenagers.
It goes without saying that bringing up children requires a lot of love, understanding and care on the one hand but also the laying down of rules and limits as well as thinking of consequences on the other (hand). So I agree with the given statement which says that children no matter how old they are must learn about limits and rules. However, I also think there must be differences in the limits set depending on the children's age.
As everyone knows, a little child, aged 5, is a lot more immature than a 15-year-old teenager. The younger one needs much more help, guidance and support because he or she can't do so many things alone. In contrast, a teenager has gained more life experience and knowledge, is more independent, has developed his/her own interests. Consequently, the adolescent needs to have fewer limits imposed on him by his parents.
Because of the lack of independence, the younger one also needs to be told what to do, and how, and what not to do when it comes to lots of other things, e.g. how to behave during breakfast time. How often do my parents tell my younger brother not to talk with his mouth full or sing or play while eating. It even gets on my nerves sometimes! There are limits which exist but he hasn't learnt to accept them. The 15-year-old knows table manners, of course.
I know how difficult it often is for parents to accept their teenage daughters or sons as individuals with their own will, ideas, attitudes, dreams and wishes. In many families, harsh arguments between parents and their children

are a part of daily life. Sometimes parents give up when kids don't play by the rules because they don't want another row. This can be a relief for some children but others need the guidance. It keeps them on the straight and narrow path.
In conclusion I want to say that there must be rules and limits for everyone and particularly for children in order for them to learn to socialize successfully. But parents must also learn to trust their children when they get older and slacken the reins. *(about 414 words)*

Lösungen zu Seite 56

1. a) My view / opinion was, that Britain is ...
   b) I agreed ...
   c) The point was ...
   d) Didn't you think that ...
   e) That was quite right ...
   f) Yes, I supposed so, but hosting the World Cup gave a great boost to tourism.
2. a) I don't feel that, either.
   b) I don't believe ...
   c) I'm not convinced ...
   d) No, perhaps you aren't right there.
   e) I don't agree with you ...

Lösungen zu Seite 58

2. – What is your favourite ... ?
   – I suppose I've got a soft spot ...
   – Isn't it rather ...
   – What do you like about ...? – Above all, ...
   – You have the impression ...
   – ... but maybe that's a good thing
   – How do you mean? – I mean ...
   – Is there anything to ... ? – Yes, plenty.
   – It's perfect for ...
   – And I gather it isn't ... ? – Well, yes and no.
   – There are many choices.
3. *Model Answer:*
   B: Well yes, but it 's extremely beautiful.
   A: What do you like most?
   B: Above all. The feeling of space, the wonderful countryside, the unusual animals, the extreme weather conditions, the history, the cities.
   A: Would you travel alone or in a group?
   B: I would travel in a group. It is more fun.
   A: Which kind of transport do you prefer?
   B: I would go by car. I believe public transport could be OK, too.

Lösungen zu Seite 59

2. *Model Answer:*
   I think fashion is a very important thing in daily life, especially for girls and women. But more and more boys and men are very interested in fashion. In my view fashion and clothes say a lot about the person wearing it. Special professions and jobs have their own dressing code.
   Businessmen cannot wear sportswear to an important meeting. A gardener should not work in his best suit.
   On the one hand clothes must be comfortable and last a very long time. On the other hand, they should look nice, too. Dressing up is fun and can also boost a person's self-esteem.

Lösungen zu Seite 60

1. a) Firstly, it damages the environment. Secondly, it costs a lot of money. Thirdly, people could use their time in a better way than waste it during rush hours.
   b) Firstly, public transport is not organised in an efficient way. Secondly, driving my own car means freedom and independence. Thirdly, no government is allowed to say no to private traffic. Mobility is one of the constitutional rights.
2. Smoking should be banned from school – Pros:
   - damage to other students' lungs
   - peer pressure may cause others to start smoking against their will
   - addiction to nicotine takes students' minds off classwork
   - students could spend their money more wisely

   The impact of television is dangerous – Pros:
   - the owner of the television station may put forward his own political views
   - children spend too much time in front of the television rather than communicating with other human beings
   - watching too much television can damage the eyes
   - people absorb information from television programmes rather than experiencing the world for themselves
   - people would be more educated if they read rather than watched television

3. a) Mixed classes should be abolished – Cons:
   - Mixed classes prepare students better for later life as they are a better reflection of society.
   - Boys and girls learn to deal with each other more naturally.
   - Boys and girls can benefit from each other's academic strength
   - Boys and girls learn to work together and understand the intricacy of the two sexes early.

   b) Violence and sex should not be shown on television – Cons:
   - it is important for people not to be sheltered from the real world, violence and sex are part of daily life
   - television is a way of informing the nation of wars and and other disturbancesat home and in other parts of the world
   - who decides what should or shouldn't be shown on television, where do you draw the line?
   - showing violence and sex can teach people what is right and what is wrong
   - why should sex always be seen as a taboo subject?

Lösungen zu Seite 61

1. – Haven't you ever looked through a fashion magazine? (Nachfrage / Lenkende Frage)
   – What about the glossy magazines which you get when you buy a Sunday newspaper? (Lenkende Frage)
   – How many people throw them straight into the dustbin? (Eher rhetorische Frage, wirkliche Antwort wird nicht erwartet)
2. *Model Answers:*
   Yes / No questions
   a) Absolutely not!
   b) Yes, I do.
   c) Don't you think a comprehensive school could be a good alternative?
   d) No, that's absolutely wrong.
   e) Definitely. Of course the government should do more against crime.
   Or Questions
   a) I would prefer private education.
   b) Don't you think it depends on the crime itself?
   c) I would prefer a co-educational school.
   d) I can't go along with sex and violence being shown on TV in the early evening.
   e) I believe going to school is like doing a job. Yes, I suppose so, but sometimes I hate my job.
3. a) In my view the increase of violence in our society is caused by the negative role of media and missing values in society.
   b) I'm convinced there are a lot of advantages to co-educational classes. Well, It is a fact men and women must work and live together later. On the other hand there are situations in mixed classes when boys or girls feel embarrassed.
   c) Sorry, I don't quite follow you.
   d) I think people can't believe in things they can't see.
   e) The programme will start next Monday because the organization has been completed.
   Negative Yes / No questions
   a) Yes, of course living together is one of the main goals of boarding schools.
   b) I do. Students of both sexes must learn together. The reason is boys and girls have to learn how to work together at school at an early age.

Lösungen zu Seite 62

1. a) a, c, d, e, g, i, j, k, l
   b) b, f, g, h, j
2. B: I'm afraid he is not in.
   B: I'm not sure when he will be back. Could I give him a message?
   B: Has Mr. Müller got your number?
   B: I'll say it again. It is 01736521412, isn't it.
   B: Could you give me your name, please?
   B: Would you spell it, please?
   B: Thanks a lot / Thank you for calling. Good bye.
3. a) A: Do you have a cellphone / mobile phone? How often do you use it?
   b) A: Who's your provider? Do you have a contract?
   c) A: Don't you think that cellphones can get on your nerves?

Lösungen zu Seite 65

1. Die folgenden Sätze sind ungeeignet, weil die Einleitungen nicht sachlich genug sind oder zu umgangssprachlich oder auch sinnlos: b, c, f, g, j, l, n, p

Lösungen zu Seite 66

1.

Expressing my opinion	Giving reasons	Agreeing	Disagreeing	Half-agreeing	Asking for clarification
In my opinion	The point is	I think so, too	I'm afraid I can't agree with you	I'd go along with	I beg your pardon
I'm convinced	It's a fact that	That's very true	That's out of the question	Don't you think that	Sorry, I don't quite follow you
		That's quite right	I can't go along with that	It seems to me that	What was that again?
			Ridiculous!	Yes perhaps you're right here	

Lösungen zu Seite 69

1. irregular, illiterate, incompetent, disunity, cyberhelmet, misinterpret, interaction, unfortunately, anti-hero, non-smoker, ex-wife, misfortune, megastar, interdependent, ex-president, internet, irrelevant, immortal, inability, indefinite, uncomfortable, coexistence, dishonest, dislike, antiseptic, impersonal, co-education, unhappy
2.

verb	***noun***	***adjective***
globalize	globalization	global
communicate	communication	communicative
talk	talker/talk	talkative
use	usefulness, usage	useful
relate	relation	relative
organize	organization	organizational
act	actor/actress	acting
weaken	weakness	weak
traumatize	trauma	traumatic
compute(rize)	computer, computerization	computerized
inform	information	informative

3. a) irregular, b) irresponsible, c) non-smoking, d) unhappy, e) misusing, f) disappeared, g) childhood, h) development, i) friendships, j) talkative, k) fashionable, l) alcoholism

Lösungen zu Seite 70 und 71

1. fills, moves, manipulates, creates, appear, sings, calls, speak, form, is gaining, is, sharing, plays, attributes, is, am going (go), are going, find, love, don't know, don't have, fall, gives, think, can't, hear, sing
2. a) are sitting, looking, are wearing, is, is; b) are you thinking about, asks; c) am thinking, miss, wonder, is doing, say, am, am getting; d) don't like, think, doesn't have; e) is working; f) asks, give, come

Lösungen zu Seite 73

1. 1. is going to, 2. is going to (goes), 3. is going to / will be living, 4. will / I am going to, 5. am going to / will, 6. will, 7. are going to, 8. will / is going to, 9. will, 10. will, 11. will, 12. is going to, 13. will, 14. will, 15. will, 16. is going to / will, 17. is going to, 18. will, 19. will, 20. will have spoken, 21. am going to / will have been, 22. will have experienced, 23. will have learnt

Lösungen zu Seite 74

2. a) She is going to live in Wallogong, New South Wales, Australia.
   b) She will see kangaroos and koalas every day.
   c) She will miss her family and friends.
   d) She is excited about going scuba diving at the Great Barrier Reef.
   e) She thinks having to speak English all the time will be difficult, but it is going to be the greatest experience she (has) ever had.
   f) She will be taking Calculus, English Literature, History and Foreign languages.
   g) Only one student, Allison, will be going / is going to Australia this year.

3. a) *Bob:* My brother and I are going to spend three weeks in the Canadian Rockies this summer.
   Tim: What are you going to do there?
   Bob: We're going to do a course in bungee jumping.
   Tim: Wow! That'll be fun!
   b) *Gavin:* Oh, I'll certainly fail my English exam.
   Emma: Don't worry so much. I'm good in English. I'll help you.
   An hour later:
   Gavin (to his mother): Emma is going to help me study for my English exam.
   c) *Mum:* Are you going to work all night? It's almost 10! You'll be very tired tomorrow if you don't stop now.
   Liz: I'll go to bed after this exercise.
   Mum: OK, I'll be back in ten minutes to see if you're in bed then.

Lösungen zu Seite 76

1. 1. took part in, 2. held, 3. was, 4. has admitted, 5. felt, 6. considered, 7. overcame, 8.have earned, 9. was confirmed, 10. won, 11. has taught, 12. has given, 13. has gained, 14. began, 15. have improved, 16. have strengthened, 17. has been, 18. have visited, 19. have had, 20. reported

Lösungen zu Seite 77

2. a) 1) has revolutionized (time until now)
   2) has been surfing ... and building (started in the past and is continuing)
   has found (indefinite time in the past)
   has gained (past action with results in the present)
   has increased (+ since: past action with results in the present)
   has developed (past action with results in the present, no definite past time indicated / still holds true)
   b) 3) a) has been carrying out, b) troubleshooting, c) building, d) has not always complied, e) has not been exploited, f) has been rewarded, g) has completed
   4) h) has been neglecting / has neglected, i) has proven, j) have been flathunting, k) has been scanning

Lösungen zu Seite 78

3. *Model Answer:*
   Reporter: Hello, my name is Anne Peters and it's a pleasure to meet you. Thank you for taking time out from your busy schedule to answer a few questions for our magazine. Right, shall we get started? When did you start writing your own songs?
   Shakira: Oh, I started writing my own songs when I was 8 years old.
   Q. Your father's Lebanese, isn't he? Have you ever visited Lebanon?
   A: Yes, my father's Lebanese and yes, I've been to Lebanon and it was thrilling. Arabic sounds have influenced my music a great deal.
   Q: Is it true that Gabriel Garcia Marquez, the famous writer, is a big fan of yours?
   A: Yes, he's a truly wonderful man who's been very encouraging.
   Q: I hear you've taken a particular interest in politics, can you comment on this?
   A: Well yes, but really this is nothing new. You see since I was born in Colombia, politics have always been very important to me. You cannot live in Colombia without being involved. Colombia has so many social problems and believe me when I say they all have to do with politics.
   Q: Have you been able to retain your Latin American creativity with your new English language songs on the Laundry Service album?
   A: Although writing in English has been a real challenge, I've managed well. I wanted to get the words right to express the themes in my songs so I spent a lot of time beforehand reading English poetry and that certainly helped.
   Q: Can we expect to hear more English songs from you?
   A: Definitely! But that doesn't mean I will not also continue to write songs in Spanish.
   Q: One final question before time runs out. When are you going to launch your next album?
   A: It will be much sooner than you think. That's all I'm saying.
   Reporter: Thank you for your time. I wish you all the best and we'll all be looking forward to your next release.
   Shakira: You're welcome, it was nice talking to you.

Lösungen zu Seite 79

4. a) was playing ... sneezed, b) was travelling ... died, c) were studying ... went off, d) was delivering ... exploded, e) began ... were ... sitting, f) was raising ... declared, g) was ... were ... nagging, h) was moving ... could ... get, i) was ... making ... shouted, j) were lining up ... made

5. *Possible Answer:*
Although Harry had never set foot in an airplane before, he joined the parachuting club in 2002. He had finally decided to face his fears instead of running away from them. Since Harry had broken his collar bone in a rugby game in 2000, he gave up/had given up sports entirely and had been spending/spent too much time alone. His friend James had suggested the whole idea of parachuting. Before the accident, Harry had always talked about someday being able to fly like a bird. Harry had refused at first, but James insisted it would do him good, get him out of his shell and had begged Harry to at least give it a try. His friend had been trying to convince him for a long time, using every tactic possible and so was thrilled when Harry eventually gave in. For almost three years until 2005, Harry had been jumping/ jumped every chance he could get. Parachuting had become his passion and whenever he went up, he felt totally exhilarated.

Lösungen zu Seite 80

6. has become
won
began
has been nominated
honoured
has belonged, sang, was
embarked, has sold
sold
8. has come ➠ came (abgeschlossene Handlung in der Vergangenheit, deshalb *simple past*)
was feeling ➠ felt (abgeschlossene Handlung; außerdem wird *feel* i. d. R. nicht in der Verlaufsform verwendet, deshalb *simple past*)
have done ➠ did (Aufzählung abgeschlossener Handlungen in der Vergangenheit, deshalb *simple past*)
always looked ➠ have always looked (beschreibt etwas in der Vergangenheit mit Bezug auf die Gegenwart; Signalwort *always*, deshalb *present perfect*)

Lösungen zu Seite 81 und 82

1. Before you jump into this, I think:
a) You should / ought to find out if your shots are up to date, especially for tetanus and hepatitis. This can / could / might save you a lot of trouble later on.
b) You really must / have to shop around before you decide on a piercing shop. There are a lot of quacks out there.
c) The piercer you finally choose should / must be qualified and experienced. You might / may want to have a look at his / her portfolio. And he absolutely has to / must wear gloves.
d) The shop itself has to / must be clean, safe and professional. There should be an autoclave for sterilizing equipment on hand.
e) The person performing the piercing has to / must thoroughly clean the area you're going to have pierced with a proper antiseptic soap. Otherwise the area might become infected.
f) The needle used must be sterilized and clean.
g) The stud must / has to be sterilized before it is attached to your lip.
h) The pierced area has to / must be cleaned.
i) Remember, the piercer should give you specific instructions on how to look after your piercing once it has been done.
j) You should know what steps need to be taken if the pierced area gets infected. I know this may sound too much but believe me, it's all for your own good.
2. Teenagers 50 years ago:
a) They had to work hard / help their parents every day.
b) At the weekend they were allowed to go to the cinema / walk in the park with their friends.
c) They weren't allowed to go to the disco every day.
d) They weren't able to play computer games or use mobile phones.
3. Life of teenagers in 50 years – *possible answers:*
a) They will be able to use the latest developments of technology.
b) They will be allowed to communicate with their friends wherever they are.
c) They will have to be careful with infectious diseases when having sex.
d) They won't be able to go swimming in clean lakes as we can do today.
e) They won't be allowed to leave the house after 9 pm because of the high crime rate in big cities.
f) They won't have to take lots of folders and textbooks to school as they will use notebooks/laptops.

Lösungen zu Seite 84 und 85

1. a) to arrive, being, call, b) to wear, keep, c) signing in, pick up, d) encouraging, to order, e) taking, check, f) eat, hurrying, g) criticizing, know, h) verify, having, pay, i) accepting, to put, divide, j) satisfying, coming back, show

2. spending, to allow, to attend, to stop, being, gyrating, distributing, enhance, not to be, taking, become, lead, clubbing, to inform, to enforce, know, curtailing, curbing, to end

Lösungen zu Seite 86

3. a) grinning, b) frightened, c) hiding, d) tearing, e) spoken, written, f) struggling, g) screaming, h) stuck, i) waiting, j) driven
4. a) I saw a little girl playing with her dog.
   b) Having read his girlfriend's e-mail, Robert phoned to thank her for the good advice she had given him.
   c) I heard my teacher talking about an idea for a new project.
   d) Sarah came home opening all the windows because of a terrible smell inside the rooms.
   e) Asked to resign because of his affair with a prostitute, the politician refused.
   f) Seeing the new CD of her favourite singer in the shop, Janet decided to buy it immediately.
   g) Susan ran to the bus stop talking to her friend on her cellphone to tell her she would be late.
   h) Anne told her employer she would work overtime if given the chance to lead the advertising campaign.
   i) Nicole Kidman, reputated to be a famous actress, is Australian.
   j) I read the book "Junk" written by Melvin Burgess.

Lösungen zu Seite 87

5. a) During my holidays I got to know an interesting American boy currently living in Berlin.
   b) I met him at a party given by his German host brother.
   c) I had heard the two boys talking about Josh's exchange year in Germany.
   d) He came/had come to Germany wanting to learn German and more about our culture.
   e) Arriving at Munich he had the feeling he would never understand any Germans.
   f) He watched a group of Bavarians talking about something he couldn't understand at all.
   g) Josh remained standing for a while thinking of/ and thought of returning home immediately.
   h) He stayed in Germany to learn the language and can speak it very well now.
   i) Although he has made lots of friends here, he is looking forward to going home.
   j) Asked if they wanted to visit Josh in the US, his host family accepted without hesitation.

Lösungen zu Seite 88 und 89

1. a) more modern, b) Better, c) (much) more, d) Less, e) worse, f) easier ... well / better, g) extremely ... highly, h) better ... more successful, i) slower, j) most important ... most needed
2. a) In high school overall grades are *mostly* based on continual assessment.
   b) Students *generally* receive what is known as credits for ...
   c) In order to graduate from high school, one has to accumulate the required number of credits *at the end of grade twelve.*
   d) *Until now,* university ... (or at end of sentence)
   e) *Moreover,* we do not have ...
   f) High school students in Germany are *seldom* given a second chance ...
   g) *Unfortunately,* Canadian tertiary institutions have higher tuition costs than German ones.
   h) Students who have completed grade twelve *successfully* can enter community colleges ...
   i) School children *at the age of 10* are *often* placed under enormous pressure *in Germany.*
3. a) A number of PISA studies show that German students don't have as good results as other European students.
   b) Unfortunately, not all students graduate from secondary school successfully.
   c) You can often find more motivated students at better equipped and more modern schools.
   d) Urgently needed reforms of the school system are only carried out quite slowly in Germany.

Lösungen zu Seite 90

1. sentences:
   a) Ben never goes to the supermarket in the evening.
   b) Kevin often spends his afternoons in the park reading a book.
   c) Jenny has been living in this wonderful town for more than 12 years now.
   d) After Alan had seen the new film, he went to bed.
   e) Although Frank was terribly ill, he came to the meeting.
   f) I phoned my friend because I wanted to know where the concert was held.
   g) They went to the cinema in order to see the new Spielberg film.
   h) While my parents were taking a walk with our dog, I was surfing the net.
   i) Have you ever seen such a fascinating show?
   j) Where did you buy the jacket I like so much?

2. *Model answers:*
   - Who did they talk to? Who did Alec play with? Who did Kate spend a wonderful day with?
   - Where did they stay? Where did they go to?
   - When did the Millers go on holiday? When did they arrive/leave Spain? When did they go to Barcelona?
   - What did they do there? What sights did Mr and Mrs Miller see? What did they eat and drink for breakfast/dinner?
   - Why didn't they arrive on time? Why didn't Mrs Miller talk to her husband on Friday?
   - How did they get there? How long did they stay there? How much money did they spend?

Lösungen zu Seite 91

1. *Model answers:*
   a) You can phone and ask me for help whenever you want to.
   b) She won't be able to solve the problem unless she asks for professional help.
   c) He had always supported her although she hardly ever thanked him.
   d) My friends were playing computer games while I was watching a new thriller.
   e) We will order some vegetarian pizzas if you don't mind.
   f) She switched on the TV in order to watch the news.
   g) He realized what mistake he had made when he read her letter.
   h) I left a message for you as you weren't at home.
   i) It was the first time I'd met him since he had gone to New York.
   j) Her parents support her financially so that she can study and care for her child.

Lösungen zu Seite 92

1. a) to, b) into, c) to, d) on / onto, e) into, f) toward, g) on / onto, h) in, into, i) on, j) to, k) on
2. a) at / beside, b) under, on, beside, between, c) under, beside, d) at / in, e) on / in, f) between, g) over

Lösungen zu Seite 93

1. a) My sister and I went to see the new Star Wars film which was one of the best films she had seen this year.
   b) Susan would really like to go to the Britney Spears concert which will be in Munich.
   c) The school books which were scattered on the floor belonged to Milton. / The school books scattered on the floor belonged to Milton.
   d) In-line skating which helps to strengthen your muscles is a great way to keep fit.
   e) My mother, who also carries on long phone conversations with her friends, is always complaining about the amount of time I spend on the telephone.
   f) Bullying which we have been having class discussions on is a serious problem in schools / We have been having class discussions on bullying which is a serious problem in many schools.
   g) Roald Dahl, whose books are appreciated by adults and children, wrote *Charlie and the Chocolate Factory.*
   h) Paul Kramer, to whom Employment Services of Disneyland, California made a part time job offer, is one of the students in our class. / Employment Services of Disneyland, California made a part time job offer to Paul Kramer one of the students in our class. / ... who is one of the students in our class.
   i) The book I am reading is *Harry Potter and the Half-Blood Prince.* / I am reading a book which is called *Harry Potter and the Half-Blood Prince.*
   j) David Beckham has a cool hairstyle, which I like a lot.

Lösungen zu Seite 94

2. a) The English course ***which*** John applied for ... / The English course ***(no relative pronoun)*** John applied for ...
   b) The lady ***who*** came into the ...
   c) *correct*
   d) He told me a story ***which / that*** I had already heard.
   e) *correct or* They were the last group ***which*** handed / ***to*** hand in.
   f) Their Geography teacher to ***whom*** they sent a letter lives in a very remote area.
   g) *correct*
   h) Sandra, ***whose*** sister has been ...
   i) Pollution in urban areas ***which*** has become ...
   j) *correct*
3. a) We can collect the tickets I ordered yesterday this evening.
   b) I read a review of the film you talked about in our newspaper.
   c) Jodie Foster, who plays the main character in *Flightplan,* was in Berlin this autumn.
   d) She plays the role as a mother of a child, who has disappeared without a trace, very well.
   e) There are people who go to the cinema just to see their favourite actors and actresses.
   f) We don't have a cinema in our town at all, which is a shame.

Lösungen zu Seite 95

1. If mum has to work this evening, I'll have to look after my baby brother.
   If I had time this evening, I would call my friend.
   If she wasn't in, I would do my maths homework instead.
   If mum had come home earlier last night, she would have made a fantastic dinner.
   If she hadn't ordered the pizza, I wouldn't have got to know the handsome pizza man.
   If he wants to see me again, he'll phone me, I'm sure.
   If dad didn't have to work so much, he would spend more time with us.
   If he has breakfast with us on Saturday, I'll tell him about my new friend.
   If he forgets my birthday, I'll never forgive him.

Lösungen zu Seite 96

2. a) did, b) will drive, c) went, d) go on, e) hadn't learned (learnt)
3. *Possible Answers:*
   a) If John ..., the school team may / will lose the championships.
   b) More members ... if we advertised more / changed the meeting time/made them more interesting / made them compulsory.
   c) I won't be ... if you can't come to my party / don't know the answer / tell me the truth.
   d) If drug dealers ... , they would be less tempted to try "pocket money" drugs / would not take so many drugs / might not become addicts.
   e) Writing letters ... if more people sent / wrote e-mails instead.
   f) The orchestra ... if the conductor didn't rehearse with them enough / didn't direct them properly.
   g) Computer technology ... if progress continues.
   h) Would you please ... have / have got some time.
   i) Olivia and Raphael ... If you both do not stop fighting right now!
   j) Do you think Sam ... if I asked him? / begged him?

Lösungen zu Seite 98

1. a) He said he was going to Dublin for the U2 Concert.
   b) He remarked he was not just seeing the band, he was helping with the show.
   c) He said he would be helping set up the stage and the light show.
   d) He pointed out it was an amazing thing and he couldn't believe it was happening to him.
   e) He said he had been following the band throughout Europe on their last tour.
   f) He said that in just under two weeks, he had seen them 10 times in 10 different cities.
   g) He remarked that at every concert he had managed to get front row tickets, although sometimes they had been really expensive.
   h) He said that after the eighth show, Bono had told him that he had seen him too many times and that he should join the road crew for the tour.
   i) He said he thought Bono had been joking with him, but he had been serious.
   j) He said he was still going to the University next year, but right now he was enjoying an experience of a lifetime.
2. a) He asked Bono when he had given his first concert.
   b) He wanted to know how they had become successful in Ireland.
   c) He asked him if he had ever thought of becoming famous before their success.
   d) He also wanted to know if he had enough time for friends despite his job.
   e) Then he asked him what his plans for the next/for the following years were.
   f) He asked him if he thought that he would still be on stage in 10 years.
   g) He asked him if he could imagine doing another job.
   h) Finally he wanted to know if he had ever been disappointed after a concert.
3. a) His mother asked him not to buy a new CD every week.
   b) She asked him to tell her when he intended to go to a concert.
   c) She warned him not to spend the night with other people he didn't know.
   d) She suggested to him to take a taxi home if the concert ended very late.
   e) She asked him to bring her an autograph of her favourite singer.

Lösungen zu Seite 99

1. a) The school is to be entered by the south doors only. All the other doors are locked until classes are over.
   b) Running in the halls is not allowed.
   c) A set of keys for all classrooms is kept by the school secretary.
   d) Classrooms must be locked by students in charge of extra-curricular activities before they leave the building.

e) School property is not to be damaged.
f) Non-marking running shoes must be worn in the gym.
g) Lockers must be used for personal belongings.
h) You are expected to be on time for your classes. Latecomers must sign in at the principal's office.
i) If you are late three times, a letter is sent home to your parents.
j) Any student caught cheating on an exam will be suspended.
k) If a student has been given a red notice, the student must have it signed by his / her parents.

Lösungen zu Seite 100

2. a) I'm sure you*'ll be asked* ...
   b) Questions on ... *can be expected.*
   c) That's right, she*'s being interviewed.*
   d) Oh yes, ... *has been conducted* ...
   e) ... applicants *were really put* through the wringer.
   f) ... while he *was being interviewed* ... / ...employees in personnel *are being put, are put under pressure/* ... documents *are not double-checked* ... / ... requirements *have to be fulfilled* ...
   g) ... to tell you what needs *to be worked on.*

Lösungen zu Seite 101

1.

sentence	***tense***	***why***
Music experts say there is a general revival of the guitar today.	simple present	genereller Fakt, auf die Gegenwart bezogen (heute)
This is changing as more and more young women are playing the guitar.	present progressive	eine gegenwärtige, vorübergehende Erscheinung; andauernder Prozess
... but recently the music scene has seen the great success of "girl bands".	simple present perfect	ein Ereignis, das erst kürzlich geschehen ist und noch Auswirkungen hat
Last year people in the UK spent £105 million on guitars.	simple past	abgeschlossene Handlung in der Vergangenheit (letztes Jahr)

Lösungen zu Seite 102

2. mögliche Antworten:

simple present	I like music a lot and often go to concerts.
present progressive	At the moment I'm listening to Robbie William's latest album.
simple present perfect	They have been a successful band for 4 years now.
simple past	My favourite girl group had their first concert in 2004.

3. a) My friend says we are a musical(ly gifted) family.
   b) My mum can sing really well and she plays the flute.
   c) My dad started to play the violin when he was five, so he is very good at it.
   d) I've been playing the guitar for two years.
   e) At the moment I'm taking piano lessons.
   f) Next month my six-year old sister is going to join a choir.

III Active/Passive

1.

active	***passive***
Last year people in the UK spent £105 million on guitars.	Ten years ago £30 million was spent on guitars in the UK.

Bildung: Form von be + past participle

2. a) Bob Dylan is regarded as one of the most important musicians of rock and pop music.
   b) Famous songs like "Knockin' On Heaven's Door" and "Like A Rolling Stone" were all written by Bob Dylan.
   c) "Blowin' In The Wind" – one of his first hits – was written in the 1960s.
   d) The first rock double album "Blonde On Blonde" was released in 1966.
   e) Another popular song from the album Desire, "Hurricane", was recorded in 1975 and released one year later in 1976.
   f) Other singers and musicians like REM, U2 and Sheryl Crow were/have been influenced by him.
   g) At the beginning of the 21st century Bob Dylan was awarded the Oscar for his composition "Things Have Changed".
   h) Surely, his songs will also be heard, played and sung in the future.

Lösungen zu Seite 103

1.

positive	*comparative*	*superlative*
famous	more famous	most famous
light	lighter	lightest
narrow	narrower	narrowest
good	better	best

2. a) A local politician can be powerful. The German chancellor is more powerful than a local politician. The US President is the most powerful person of the three.
   b) A record player is more modern than a gramophone, but the CD-player is the most modern way of listening to music.
   c) An autograph can be interesting. An interview is usually more interesting. The most interesting thing is a live concert.
   d) A crossword puzzle can be difficult. A test is more difficult. An exam is the most difficult thing of the three.

V Modal auxiliaries

1. a) Second you **have to** practise.
   b) If you **can't**, or don't have the money to pay for lessons, then you **can** use a book or just learn to play your favourite songs.
   c) Third, you **should** find a band.
2.

modal auxiliaries	*substitutes*
can	be able to
can, may	be allowed to
must	have to

3. a) As a child I **couldn't/wasn't allowed to/wasn't able to** go to concerts of my favourite bands.
   b) But since I liked music a lot, I **could/was able to** play simple songs on the guitar at the age of eight.
   c) In order to learn how to play more musical instruments I **had to/was allowed to** attend music school twice a week.
   d) Today I **cannot** only play five different instruments, I also have my own band.

Lösungen zu Seite 104

1. a) past participle *anstelle eines Relativsatzes:* Five years ago in the US, Tish Ciravolo, a bass guitar player, set up the first company to produce guitars which are made for girls.
   b) present participle *anstelle eines Relativsatzes:* Tish says, "What I wanted to do was not only design a guitar for a girl to play, but to change the consciousness – make the sight of a girl who is playing the guitar as natural as that of a girl who is playing the flute.
   c) gerund *nach Präposition*
2. a) Last week Britney bought a guitar offered for £ 160 in a music shop in London.
   b) She had watched the shop assistant showing different flutes to a woman and her child.
   c) Having bought the new instrument she wanted to try it out immediately. After buying ...
   d) At the moment Britney is sitting in her bedroom playing her new guitar.

VII Relative Clauses

1. A piano is a large musical instrument with lots of black and white keys and which is similar to a keyboard. A concert is a musical event / performance which is visited by lots of people who come to listen to one or several musicians or singers. A song is a text which can rhyme and is usually sung. A guitarist is a person who plays the guitar. An orchestra is a large group of musicians playing different kinds of instruments. A CD is a small plastic disc on which data like music can be stored and you can put it in a CD player to listen to it.

VIII Conditional Clauses

1. *Conditional Typ I*
2. 1. C (III), 2. D (III), 3. E (I), 4. A (II), 5. B (I)

Lösungen zu Seite 106

1. Megan said that her life had become really dark. Huffing had been a way to get out of her head. It kind of had numbed her.
   She had known that her mum wouldn't know what huffing was/had been. And it had been easy to hide because she had been using products from the house.

It was/is more effective if kids heard/hear about huffing from someone their own age. She told them it wasn't/isn't worth ruining their life for a 15-minute high.

2. How old were you when you tried huffing for the first time?
   How did it make you feel?
   What products for inhaling did you use and how did you get them?
   Why did you start huffing and what do you know about other kids' reasons?
   What made you change your mind on huffing?
   What was it like in the treatment center?

Lösungen zu Seite 107

3.

Example	*Tense*	*Explanation*
She was hanging out with six friends after school, when one of them took out an aerosol can, sprayed it onto a towel and breathed it. (ll. 3–8)	1) past progressive 2) and 4) simple past	1) Hintergrundhandlung, Handlung im Verlauf 2) neu hinzukommende Handlung und aufeinanderfolgende Handlungen
Two months later Megan, who lives in Watertown, South Dakota, was addicted to inhalants. (ll. 20–23)	1) simple present 2) simple past	1) Fakt in der Gegenwart 2) abgeschlossene Handlung in der Vergangenheit
"We all had used huffing to solve our problems." (ll. 89–91)	simple past perfect	Handlung, die noch vor einer anderen Handlung (Therapie in der Gruppe) in der Vergangenheit passiert war
She's been clean now for more than two years, but Megan admits it hasn't been easy. (ll. 94–97)	1) simple present perfect 2) simple present 3) simple present perfect	1) Zustand, der in der Vergangenheit begonnen hat und bis zur Gegenwart andauert 2) Gegenwart 3) Zustand, der in der Vergangenheit begonnen hat und bis zur Gegenwart andauert
"It's more effective if kids hear about huffing from someone their own age." (ll. 102–104)	simple present	genereller Fakt – Gegenwart

4. a) summary writing:
   The text "Special Report: teens and drugs in America" deals with the problem of huffing among young teens in the US. It describes how 12-year-old Megan starts huffing together with some friends, which she sees as a way of forgetting about a bad experience. When her addiction and pain become worse after some time, she takes pills and is found in a bad state by her mother and taken to the emergency room. When her parents get to know about her addiction, they take her to a treatment center where she gets clean and starts helping other teens with the same problems telling about her own experience. Megan has been clean for more than two years now, which hasn't been easy as lots of her friends still huff.
   (128 words)

   b) comment writing:
   Drug taking including the use of inhalants, smoking, drinking alcohol as well as using soft drugs like hash is still a problem in our society. Also some young people take drugs in order to get "high", i.e. to forget about their problems, at least for some time. But is this worth risking your life for? I don't think so and want to show that there are lots of reasons against it.
   Of course, life is not always easy and lots of us have problems which we would like to forget. Drugs – or inhalants for those who can't or don't want to afford drugs – are seen as a means to escape from reality and forget about problems. Unfortunately the intended good feeling doesn't last for a long time unless you increase the drug intake and thus your addiction. One shouldn't forget that inhalants could/can be even lethal or at least cause serious health problems as other drugs do.
   Personally I believe there is hardly any problem that is so bad that you would wish to die. Consequently, one should never forget the potential dangers of huffing or other drugs. On the contrary, we must learn how to cope with problems and solve them even if it means seeking professional help.
   In short, don't risk your life by taking any drugs. Enjoy it and accept that there are ups and downs in everybody's life, otherwise it would be boring.
   (229 words)

OKiDOKi Lernhilfen
Die Neubearbeitung:
Alle Bände 96 Seiten, vierfarbig

Deutsch

Deutsch Rechtschreiben Kl. 5
3-507-22205-1

Deutsch Aufsätze schreiben Kl. 5
3-507-22209-4

Deutsch Grammatik Kl. 5/6
3-507-22206-X

Deutsch Rechtschreiben Kl. 6
3-507-22207-8

Deutsch Aufsätze schreiben Kl. 6
3-507-22212-4

Deutsch Rechtschreiben Kl. 7
3-507-22210-8

Deutsch Aufsätze schreiben Kl. 7
3-507-22213-2

Deutsch Rechtschreiben Kl. 8
3-507-22211-6

Deutsch Aufsätze schreiben Kl. 8
3-507-22214-0

Fremdsprachen

Englisch Wortschatz Kl. 5
3-507-22230-2

Englisch Grammatik Kl. 5
3-507-22231-0

Englisch Wortschatz Kl. 6
3-507-22232-9

Englisch Grammatik Kl. 6
3-507-22233-7

Englisch Wortschatz Kl. 7
3-507-22234-5

Englisch Grammatik Kl. 7
3-507-22235-3

Englisch Wortschatz Kl. 8
3-507-22236-5

Englisch Grammatik Kl. 8
3-507-22237-X

Französisch, 1. Lernjahr
3-507-22281-7

Französisch, 2. Lernjahr
3-507-22282-5

Französisch, 3. Lernjahr
3-507-22183-3

Spanisch, 1. Lernjahr
3-507-22240-X

Spanisch, 2. Lernjahr
3-507-22245-0

2 in 1
Zum Nachschlagen

Alle Bände 32 Tafeln, vierfarbig

Deutsche Grammatik
Kl. 5–10
3-507-22285-X

Rechtschreibung und Zeichensetzung Kl. 5–10
3-507-22286-8

Englische Grammatik
Kl. 5–10
3-507-22287-6

Französische Grammatik
Kl. 7-10
3-507-22288-4

Spanische Grammatik
Kl. 7-10
3-507-22289-2

Mathematik Algebra
3-507-22290-6

Mathematik Geometrie
3-507-22291-4

OKiDOKi FiT iN ...

Alle Bände 132 Seiten, vierfarbig

Deutsch

FiT iN Deutsch
für den Übergang in die weiterführende Schule
3-507-22250-7

FiT iN Deutsch
für den Übergang von Klasse 6 in Klasse 7
3-507-22251-5

FiT iN Deutsch für den Abschluss nach Klasse 10
3-507-22252-3

FiT iN Deutsch für den Übergang in die Sekundarstufe II
3-507-22253-1

Mathematik

FiT iN Mathematik
für den Übergang in die weiterführende Schule
3-507-22260-4

FiT iN Mathematik
für den Übergang von Klasse 6 in Klasse 7
3-507-22261-2

FiT iN Mathematik
für den Übergang in die Sekundarstufe II
3-507-22263-9

Englisch

FiT iN Englisch für den Übergang von Klasse 6 in Klasse 7
3-507-22271-X

FiT iN Englisch für den Übergang in die Sekundarstufe II
3-507-22273-6